Reading: Implementing the Bullock Report

Proceedings of the fourteenth annual course and conference of the United Kingdom Reading Association, Avery Hill College, London, 1977

Editors
Elizabeth Hunter-Grundin
and
Hans U. Grundin

Ward Lock Educational

ISBN 0 7062 3712 9

First published 1978

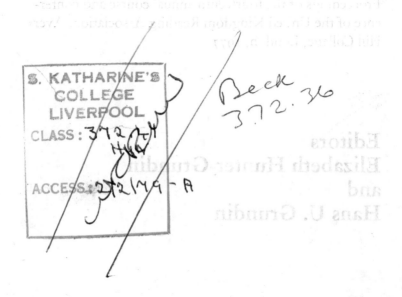

Beck
372.36

Set in 11 on 13 point Garamond and printed by
Latimer Trend & Company Ltd for
Ward Lock Educational
116 Baker Street, London W1M 2BB
A member of the Pentos Group
Made in Great Britain

Contents

Foreword

The fourteenth annual study conference of the United Kingdom Reading Association was held at Avery Hill College in London, from 25–9 July, 1977. At the Reception, delegates were welcomed by Peter Newsam, Chief Education Officer of the Inner London Education Authority.

The conference focused on implementation of the Bullock Report recommendations, which are sufficiently universal to be of interest to delegates from abroad who contributed significantly to the success of the conference.

In terms of outcome, perhaps the most interesting feature of the conference is the series of recommendations listed in Part 4 of this volume. Almost all of the delegates were active in one of the eleven working parties, and in the brief time available to them they accomplished the valuable task of defining, discussing and modifying recommendations which merit the earnest attention of the educational agencies to which they are addressed. It is therefore with special emphasis that I wish to thank each and every one of the delegates for their contributions.

As always, the Publishers' Exhibition was an important feature of the conference, and I wish to thank the many editors and publishers' representatives who were with us this year.

Traditionally, lecturers at our conferences receive neither fees nor recompense for travel or other expenses incurred. The quality of this year's programme was in itself tangible proof of the generosity and dedication of those educationists who took part in it, and on behalf of the UKRA membership, I wish to thank them most sincerely.

Elizabeth Hunter-Grundin
President, 1976–77

Introduction: The Bullock Report, and then . . .

Elizabeth Hunter-Grundin

In February 1975 the Department of Education and Science published a volume entitled *A Language for Life*. This was the report of a committee of inquiry appointed by the Secretary of State for Education and Science, under the chairmanship of Sir Alan Bullock (now Lord Bullock). All references within this book to the 'Bullock Report' are references to *A Language for Life* – and not to the later Bullock Report on industrial relations.

'Our' Bullock Committee was set up as a result of a report published in 1972 by the National Foundation for Educational Research, which indicated that standards of literacy among school children were less than satisfactory. The Committee's terms of reference were:

to consider in relation to schools
(a) all aspects of teaching the use of English, including reading, writing and speech;
(b) how present practice might be improved and the role that initial and in-service training might play;
(c) to what extent arrangements for monitoring the general level of attainment in these skills can be introduced or improved;
and to make recommendations.

The Committee summarized the result of its work in 333 conclusions and recommendations, which were further condensed into the following seventeen principal recommendations:

1   A system of monitoring should be introduced which will employ new instruments to assess a wider range of attain-

ments than has been attempted in the past and allow new criteria to be established for the definition of literacy.

2 There should be positive steps to develop the language ability of children in the preschool and nursery and infant years. These should include arrangements for the involvement of parents, the improvement of staffing ratios in infant schools, and the employment of teachers' aides whose training has included a language element.

3 Every school should devise a systematic policy for the development of reading competence in pupils of all ages and ability levels.

4 Each school should have an organized policy for language across the curriculum, establishing every teacher's involvement in language and reading development throughout the years of schooling.

5 Every school should have a suitably qualified teacher with responsibility for advising and supporting his colleagues in language and the teaching of reading.

6 There should be close consultation between schools, and the transmission of effective records, to ensure continuity in the teaching of reading and in the language development of every pupil.

7 English in the secondary school should have improved resources in terms of staffing, accommodation, and ancillary help.

8 Every LEA should appoint a specialist English adviser and should establish an advisory team with the specific responsibility of supporting schools in all aspects of language in education.

9 LEAs and schools should introduce early screening procedures to prevent cumulative language and reading failure and to guarantee individual diagnosis and treatment.

10 Additional assistance should be given to children retarded in reading, and where it is the school's policy to withdraw pupils from their classes for special help they should continue to receive support at the appropriate level on their return.

11 There should be a reading clinic or remedial centre in every LEA, giving access to a comprehensive diagnostic service and

expert medical, psychological, and teaching help. In addition to its provision for children with severe reading difficulties, the centre should offer an advisory service to schools in association with the LEA's specialist adviser.

12 Provision for the tuition of adult illiterates and semiliterates should be greatly increased, and there should be a national reference point for the coordination of information and support.

13 Children of families of overseas origin should have more substantial and sustained tuition in English. Advisers and specialist teachers are required in greater strength in areas of need.

14 A standing working party should be formed, made up of representatives of the DES and LEAs, to consider capitation allowances and the resources of schools, and a satisfactory level of book provision should be its first subject of inquiry.

15 A substantial course on language in education (including reading) should be part of every primary and secondary school teacher's initial training, whatever the teacher's subject or the age of the children with whom he or she will be working.

16 There should be an expansion in in-service education opportunities in reading and the various other aspects of the teaching of English, and these should include courses at diploma and higher degree level. Teachers in every LEA should have access to a language/reading centre.

17 There should be a national centre for language in education, concerned with the teaching of English in all its aspects, from language and reading in the early years to advanced studies with sixth forms.

The third of these principal recommendations, namely that 'Every school should devise a systematic policy for the development of reading competence in pupils of *all ages and ability levels*' (my italics), was particularly welcomed by those of us who deplored the still widely-held belief that reading should be taught in the infant school and thereafter only in cases where 'remedial' teaching was deemed necessary. It is, of course, manifest nonsense to suggest that any child, however well taught or intellectually gifted, should at the age of seven or eight have reached a level of attainment in reading which requires no further improvement. But the fact remains that the majority of the school population of 'average' or 'above average' young people receive no systematic teaching aimed at the improvement of their reading skills after the age of seven or eight years. It is very rarely that one meets a student entering the field of higher education who has had the benefits of any kind of course in reading and study skills in preparation for examinations at 'O' or 'A' level. Even now, in what can be called the post-Bullock era, there is little evidence to suggest that the Report has had much influence on the school curriculum. To cite only one example, few educationists, if any, would question the desirability of curriculum revision to create more emphasis on study skills (library, reference, access, note-taking skills, etc.) at the secondary school level. We hardly need the Bullock Report to remind us that training in these skills should be part of every secondary school's 'systematic policy'. Why, then, does it remain an area of curriculum neglect?

In this, as in many other areas of neglect, there is little doubt that apathy and inertia are largely to blame. But whose apathy and inertia? It is difficult to know precisely where the omission or neglect has its source. Teachers tend to teach as they themselves have been taught, and it is unlikely that many of them were ever taught how to abstract necessary information from a textbook with maximum efficiency and it should, in all fairness, be pointed out that most teachers claim – and with a great deal of justification – that they were never trained to teach reading in the first place.

Heads of schools and heads of English departments within schools tend to confine their attention to administrative and disciplinary matters, and without underestimating the importance or the time-consuming nature of these tasks, it must be recognized that they bear little relation to the basic problems of the language and reading curriculum. Local Education Authority advisory staff are usually too few in number to make any real impact, and they are rarely empowered to initiate significant changes in the curriculum. Their only means of influencing the situation seems to be to organize courses for a small percentage of the teachers and hope that they will pass the 'message' on to their colleagues. Her

4

Majesty's Inspectors are even fewer in number and have even less power to influence what is taught in schools, restricted as they are by protocol and by the Local Education Authorities' tendency to mistrust anything that may be construed as central government influence over the educational system in general and the curriculum in particular.

In February 1976, the *Times Educational Supplement* published the results of a survey entitled 'Bullock Plus One'. This was an attempt to summarize the effects of the Report during the first year after its publication. The evidence was far from optimistic. Some of the more enterprising Local Education Authorities had launched campaigns of in-service courses, while others only paid lip-service to the principal Bullock Report recommendations by arranging a day conference. We were told in the TES survey that 33,547 teachers had attended conferences (of some kind!) on the Bullock Report and its recommendations. Like all large numbers this seems very impressive, but it becomes much less so when we realize that this impressive number only constitutes a little more than 5 per cent of the teachers concerned with the Bullock Report, i.e. *all* teachers. But more disturbing than the failure to involve even a substantial minority in the discussions, is the lack of any evidence of *implementation* – of curriculum change resulting from some of the 333 conclusions and recommendations underpinned by data from within the 609 pages of the Report.

There is little doubt that the Bullock Report is failing to stimulate the special kind of interest and energy required to bring about significant curriculum change. Perhaps the Report was too lengthy, its terms of reference too extensive? Perhaps it was too theoretical? Were practitioners disenchanted by statements like 'there is no one method, medium, approach, device, or philosophy that holds the key to the process of learning to read'? Did we expect, if not 609 pages of magic formulae to cure all illnesses of the curriculum, at least more straightforward prescriptions for action at the level of the individual school and the classroom?

There is not much point in speculating about what went wrong with the Bullock Report, or with the way in which it was first received. The important thing is to note that the immense problem is here – in many ways eminently analysed and defined by the Bullock Committee – and that the daunting task of solving it still faces us. Perhaps the most serious weakness of the Bullock Report is that it tends to be conceived as an end-product, rather than as a beginning. Great effort went into the creation of this impressive volume, and it is natural if, having finished it, those responsible drew a sigh of relief and said: 'That's it!' with the result that the Report stands on bookshelves up and down the country as the Definitive Report. But where do we go from here?

The Secretary to the Bullock Committee, Ron Arnold, has said that as far as he was concerned it was 'a life for language' to work on *A Language for Life*. I think that in stating his personal feelings *vis-à-vis* the enormous task, he also put his finger on an important limitation in the Committee's work. The task taken on by the Bullock Committee was, indeed, a task for life, or even a never-ending one, since in being a 'life-long' task for the whole system of education, its time span must far exceed the life span of any individual.

In view of the need for a continuous effort to solve and continuously improve our solutions to the problems tackled by the Bullock Committee, it seemed to me imperative that the 14th Annual Study Conference of the United Kingdom Reading Association, for which I as President of the Association was responsible, should make a contribution towards this end. I therefore decided to give it a clear focus in choosing as the Conference theme: 'Reading: Curriculum Demands – Implementing the Bullock Report'.

The annual UKRA Conference brings together our most eminent educationists in the field of language and literacy, and a lot of expertise and effort goes into the preparation of contributions. The decision to focus the entire Conference on this theme enabled us to concentrate considerable intellectual resources on this attempt to contribute to the solution of the problems discussed by the Bullock Committee.

The Conference was held at Avery Hill College in London, from 25–9 July 1977, and in its many valuable sessions a large number of papers was presented. The papers included in this volume are only a selection of those read at the Conference. These papers and the recommendations of the working parties (Part 4) provide, I hope, the kind of outcome from which further progress can be developed.

Part 1

Setting the scene

1 Reading for life: the psycholinguistic base

Kenneth S. Goodman, Yetta M. Goodman and
Carolyn Burke

Perhaps it is because the English language has achieved world-
wide scope and diversity that scholars from all parts of the
English-speaking world are coming to see the dynamic interrelationship of language, culture and learning. They are seeing language as an ever-changing process which expands and grows
throughout the life of individuals and communities. *A Language
for Life*, the Bullock Report, admirably represents that view.

Certainly it is true that in our growing understanding of reading
as a language process, major contributions have come from
Britain, Scotland, Australia, New Zealand, Canada and the United
States. If this effort has been international, it has also been inter-
disciplinary, an integration of work in education, in linguistics, in
psychology, in sociology and anthropology and in the new cross
disciplines, psycholinguistics, sociolinguistics, and educational
linguistics.

To understand reading and to build sound programmes for
literacy development, it is necessary to put reading into both a
language and personal sociocultural context. In *A Language for
Life* the Bullock Committee recognized that language is not an
end in itself or a sterile, static subject for study in school, but
rather the means and medium of human communication, an
essential of personal and social life. Reading, as a language
process, must also be seen as an essential aspect of life in a
literate society.

In this paper we will present a model of reading that results
from viewing it from these vantage points. We will present a brief
view of the ontogeny of reading. And we will present our view
of the alternate instructional models that are possible and how
they relate to the goals of reading for life.

We begin then by stating a simple premise. Reading is language. Language has two aspects – productive and receptive. It is always an interaction between the producer and the receiver. Both are interactive participants in communication. Receptive language is no less active than productive language. In oral language the participants are speaker and listener. In written language they are writer and reader. So reading is a receptive written language process, one in which the reader constructs meaning, actively, from a printed display authored by a writer. Though the participants are separated in time and space, reading is no less an interactive process than listening to someone in a face-to-face situation.

Two decades of scholarship in language have made it clear that it is perhaps the most human of human characteristics. It differentiates us most from other living species. We use language not only to communicate but as a medium of thought and learning. As Halliday (1971) has said, learning language is also learning how to mean. In fact, function, the need to use language to express certain needs, precedes the development and is a necessary prerequisite for developing control of the form of language. Language is the essential for survival for humans, born dependent, in human society. Control of language is the means for such survival.

All human societies have language. Not all have written language. Some have interpreted this fact to mean that written language is unlike oral language or at least not learned like oral language. But what it really reflects is the relationship of linguistic form and function in a social context. Oral language is sufficient for communication of hearing people in small self-contained communities. When the society and culture become complex to the point that people must preserve communication over time and communicate over space, then written language is developed. It is developed anew or it is developed by adaptation of the written forms of other societies. The particular uses made of written language make it differ from oral language more in form than in function. But even in function, written language shows some differences because it is more likely to be outside of the situational context which accompanies most oral language. Writers must be more complete in expressing their meanings and must use language to create contexts which the situation provides for listeners.

We have described the model we are presenting here as psycholinguistic, because there is an interaction between language and thought as the reader seeks to construct meaning from print. It is meaning and not language which preoccupies the reader. Yet the reader must use language as the base for constructing meaning. The model we present is, of course, theoretical. Theory is necessary in reading for the generation of questions and hypotheses for research, as a means of tying together the findings of research on how reading works, how it is taught, how it is learned. Theory is necessary as a solid base on which to build methods and materials for instruction and for evaluation of reading effectiveness. Reading, like all language processes, only exists in use. Since its use always relates to meaning, any productive discussion of the reading process must be within the context of real readers actively attempting to construct meaning.

Three cue systems

Readers use three cue systems which we can separate for the sake of discussion but which are always in integral relationship to each other in actual language use:

1 In an alphabetic writing system, the *grapho-phonic system* includes the distinctive features of letters and spelling patterns which make up the orthography of the written language, the sound system or phonology, and the phonic system which we define as the relationships between orthography and phonology of the language.
2 The *syntactic system* includes the surface structures, grammatical rules and deep structures of the language itself. In reading and listening as receptive processes, the language user is responding to the surface representation and supplying the rest of the grammar.
3 The *semantic system* of cues is the meaning itself. It depends directly on the experiences and conceptual development of the reader; that is, meaning is input by the reader as well as output from reading. Readers make use of linguistic and conceptual schema as they read.

Six strategies in reading

Readers use some psycholinguistic strategies to achieve efficiency and effectiveness in reading. All operate in one or more of the reading cycles we discuss below:

1 *Recognition*. To evoke appropriate strategies for reading, the readers must recognize a task as a reading task. They must sort out and give particular attention to written language in a busy visual environment. They must further recognize certain particular characteristics of the written language, that it is in cursive form, for example. Bilinguals must recognize which language is involved.

2 *Sampling*. Efficient language processing requires that the reader sample from the visual display, choosing the cues which will provide the most useful and dependable information. A key principle in receptive language is that economy requires using the least amount of information necessary to get effectively to meaning.

3 *Predicting*. Anticipation is a key strength of human cognitive processing. We are able to anticipate what has not yet been observed by applying schema we have developed through past experience and learning. Prediction is also a vital strategy in reading. Readers are engaged in a continuous guessing game as they predict meaning, syntactic structures, and graphophonic elements and patterns. The cues sampled serve the double purpose of being the basis of predictions as well as the confirmation of prior predictions.

4 *Confirming*. Since readers sample and predict they must monitor their own progress. They do this by constantly checking to see if what they have predicted is supported by further reading and by whether they are able to make sense of what they have already processed. If they get confirmation they proceed, if not then they must correct.

5 *Correcting*. When the readers detect an inconsistency or are unable to make sense of what they are reading, then they must use correction strategies to reprocess, regress, gather more information, and otherwise recover meaning.

6 *Terminating*. Finally, readers must be able to terminate when they are finished reading or when the reading ceases to be productive. Termination is a strategy that adults use frequently but school children are not always permitted to use.

Four cycles in reading

Reading may be considered a cyclical process which shifts from centering on the print display to ultimate construction of meaning. Each of the four cycles spirals into the next and since meaning is the goal the reader leaps towards meaning without necessarily fully completing each cycle. The six strategies are used in varying ways during the four cycles. Memory, both short and long term, is continuously supplying and storing information during reading.

1 *The optical cycle.* Since reading utilizes the eyes as its principle input medium, reading has an optical cycle. The eyes focus their lenses on fixation points on the page and sweep from fixation to fixation utilizing input in both sharp and fuzzy areas of the visual field. In this optical cycle, it must be remembered that the brain and not the eye controls human information processing. The eye uses its optical systems but it does so at the direction of the brain which predicts where the most useful information will be before the eye has focused.

2 *The perceptual cycle.* The brain has the ability to use two eyes not only while at rest, but also as the head and body move, to create a single visual impression which appears to stay in continuous focus. The perceptual process this involves depends very much on what is known and anticipated by the reader. What we see is largely what we have predicted we will see and what we are prepared to see. In this cycle the reader uses sampling strategies in confirming predictions and in making new predictions. Images are created which are checked against prior decoding, against current prediction, and against semantic and syntactic acceptability.

3 *The syntactic cycle.* Language has a structure, grammar, which makes it possible for it to express comprehensibly any human thought or experience. In receptive language, readers must assign a structure as they begin to process a sentence and determine the clauses and the relationships between them to get to meaning. Sometimes those syntactic predictions are made with a high degree of confidence; sometimes they are very tentative. In either case, readers monitor to make sure that further sampling confirms their predictions. Disconfirmation brings regressing, reprocessing and correction.

4   *The semantic cycle.* Readers can only be said to be decoding when they go from language, a coded representation, to meaning. As reading progresses a semantic context is created which makes further predictions (grapho-phonic, syntactic and semantic) more constrained. Uncertainty is reduced, but the process of constructing meaning is not simply additive. New meaning must be assimilated and meaning stored in memory must be accommodated.

In any case it is the search for meaning, the active continuous attempt to comprehend, that makes all of this complex process work. What distinguishes more and less proficient reading is how well integrated it is: how efficiently and effectively cues of all sorts are used, strategies applied, and meaning created.

All reading, however, good and bad, mature or immature, utilizes this process. At all levels of development in all languages, the only real difference is how well it is all brought together.

Ontogeny of reading

Many of our colleagues have been supportive of our model of reading as a psycholinguistic guessing game. 'Probably,' they say, 'it's a model which might very well describe the developing reader, but certainly that's not how kids learn to read. A carefully controlled language programme is necessary at the beginning stages.'

We decided to find out more about the onset of learning to read. Since all of our work suggests that processing written language is similar to processing oral language we looked to the scientists of oral language development to help us understand more about the development of written language.

In order to understand the beginnings of oral language development, linguists and psycholinguists decided to study the roots of language learning in two, three and four year olds. They were amazed at what young children know about language at such an age. Psychologists are at the present time looking at even younger children to gain deeper insights into the process.

Since our view of reading suggests that a reader is an active participant in learning to read, we began to wonder about the emergence of reading. We examined the work of an international group of scholars – Jessie Reid, Marie Clay, Frank Smith, John Downing, Ragnhild Söderbergh and Charles Read. A number of questions began to plague us: Is it possible that in a print-oriented society children develop awareness of the nature of print at the ages of two, three and four? Is it possible that most children learn to read in some sense prior to schooling? Is it possible that researchers have not discovered this early learning of written language because the behaviour is going on in the child's head and there is little overt manifestation that it is happening?

We began to do some research with two, three, and four year old children. We used print which was familiar to them from television, the streets, the motorways, the supermarkets. From our investigations we have come to some tentative conclusions.

Children are learning to read by themselves as they interact with print at the ages of two, three, and four. This happens only in print-oriented societies and cultures where print bombards the visual sense of children. Think of the streets and markets which preschoolers walk through. Television commercials can be a source of this bombardment as well. Children must learn to organize the print in their environment as they learn to organize the rest of their world. In a similar way that they learn to understand how four-legged animals differ from two-legged animals, they learn that print says something while pictures have other kinds of functions. Early in our research, we realized that when preschoolers pointed to print, they would ask 'what does that *say*?' This seems to suggest an awareness on the child's part that print is communicative – it conveys meaning. It is at this point of awareness that reading begins. Beginning reading at this stage is not alphabetic. Children are aware that print does the telling, but reading is an act of meaning. Therefore, the cut-out front panel of *Rice Krispies* is cereal, the *Crest* panel is toothpaste and *Pepsi-Cola* can be called Coke. The child is usually aware of the appropriate category. Print within its context tells you what something says; it is a symbol like an ideograph. Understanding the alphabetic nature of written language comes later. This supports Halliday's notion that form follows function.

Preschoolers are using a variety of cueing systems as they read: just as proficient readers do, they use the print and the meaning. In addition, they use pictorial cues including colour and the situational context. Not only do they use these cues as they respond to print, but they bring cues from their own background and experience to construct meaning. Given a cut-out front from a *Macdonald's French Fries* envelope, one child yelled – 'that's *Macdonald's French Fries'*. She only had a two dimensional form but could construct what the whole was from her previous experiences. 'Where does it say *Macdonald's French Fries*?', we ask, and the child points to the small black bold-face letters, moving her finger from right to left saying *'Macdonald's French Fries'* quickly and moving her finger slowly so it all comes out even. She could have pointed to a whole line of golden arches. The child is using the whole situation to construct meaning but knows it is the print that does the telling or saying of the meaning. One more example can support this point. We have a magazine picture of a large automobile. As the picture comes in view, our subjects most often say *car*. 'Where does it say *car*?' we ask. Our subjects again quickly will respond by finding a very small printed *Chevrolet* in the upper-left-hand corner and moving their fingers back and forth across the word.

When print is totally decontextualized, preschoolers no longer treat it as meaningful language. For example, given a wrapper pasted on a cardboard which says IVORY in large blue letters on a design of blue and white wavy lines in the background, there is enough context so that almost all of our three and four year olds respond with either *soap* or *Ivory*. When the same word IVORY is printed in manuscript form our subjects react in three different ways. Some respond immediately with, 'You know I can't read.' Others start naming the letters often incorrectly. One four year old who read *Ivory* in the contextualized task, pointed to each letter saying, 'one, v, zero, r, y'. The third group acted bored, fidgety or silly. Being able to read in situationally-embedded contexts but not out of them is very like oral language development.

Lois Bloom (1970) says:

Children talk about events that are immediately, perceptually available in the nonlinguistic context – adults do not talk about what they see and what they are doing when a listener is there to see for himself. It appears that child utterances depend directly on the support of nonlinguistic context whereas adult utterances do not.

Children make use of all the reading strategies as described by the model.

Early on, readers recognize print and select the cues they believe to be significant. One four-year-old subject, upon seeing a label from *Chicken of the Sea Tuna* said, 'That's *chicken*! No, tuna! No, dog food!' The first cue was the print *Chicken*; she then realized it was not really chicken by picking up additional cues. We are not sure which ones. We could not understand the reason for the 'dog food' response until one of us noticed a red-and-white-checked symbol on the can which is the symbol used by the Ralston Purina Company, the manufacturer of a large line of dog food in the US, which also manufactures *Chicken of the Sea Tuna*. With a lot of experience with a variety of print in many different situations, readers learn which are the significant language cues and which are not. It is very important in language learning to be selective. Our early readers show they are beginning to do this! Children constantly are predicting on the basis of experiences. Their responses to print in these early stages are almost never random as in the *Chicken of the Sea* example. There is evidence of self-correction as the emergent reader rejects alternatives on the basis of additional cues or because something does not seem to make sense. The *Chicken of the Sea* example supports the use of this strategy. Another example comes from a four year old who responded to the picture of the *Chevrolet* car mentioned earlier, by saying, 'Bruick'. 'Where does it say Bruick? 'the researcher asked. He pointed to the small print and said, 'No, it's a *Cadillac*, no, that's a *Chevette*. I thought it was a Bruick 'cause my auntie drives one.' Through all of these examples, it is obvious that young beginning readers are making sense out of print.

Young language learners are tentative. They begin to form generalizations about the alphabetic nature of print and often realize when they do not know. Three year olds are often quick to 'read' *Rice Krispies* as *cereal*, while five year olds respond more slowly. Most often they respond with, 'I don't know', but when gently encouraged to guess, some say, 'It's not *Raisin Bran*' or, 'I know it's some kind of cereal'. These children are at a more mature stage in terms of written language development. They are beginning to relate sound to letters. Yet their initial responses suggest that they know less than some three year olds.

Another caution is that children are developing concepts about print but the labels they use may not be appropriate. Although in responding to print in context, four year olds usually respond with a two-word response for a two-word text item, they will use the terms *word, letter, number* interchangeably. What's important to realize is that these terms are all conceptually related. In addition, children can frequently use language in an appropriate context, although when asked to define the same item, they cannot do so. Part of the task we have given our readers is a book-knowledge task. We hold up a *page* in a book, wave it back and forth and say, 'What is this?' None of the twelve three and four year olds last tested could answer the question. However, as the researcher read them a story and came to the end of the print on the page and said, 'What should I do now?', every one of the children replied, 'Turn the *page*.'

Children all seem to respond easily and appropriately to print in environmental settings. They know stop signs, the food they eat, the TV programmes they watch. This does not automatically prepare them for knowledge of books. Print in the environmental world seems to be more universally known by children than the function of print in books. Again we see the model of reading at work. Children bring their own background and experiences to their reading.

Alternative models of reading instruction
If we define language as being both *natural* and learned we then arrive at the key pedagogical question. What set of experiences and materials will best support a student's development of reading as an expression of language?

We believe that most instruction revolves around some notion of *predictability*. Everyone who sets out to instruct or to produce instructional materials makes some initial assumptions concerning what the student already knows and the organization of the process which is to be learned. Everyone assumes that what is to be learned must be encountered by the student in some form which will be found logical and understandable – that is predictable.

This is why so many of us in reading, of so many different theoretical stripes, can find ourselves chorusing Dewey's admonition that instruction must start where the child is.

We can agree on this point and yet disagree upon what the actual instruction should be. This disagreement arises out of different notions of what the child knows, of the ways in which the child comes to know, and of how the reading process is organized. We can agree on the need for predictability and yet disagree on what is predictable.

Let us explore the effect which varying notions of reading process organization can have upon instruction and upon instructional materials. One old view of reading sees it as an appendage to speech with the main task of the reader being to recode the print into speech. This phonics model of reading can be pictured as a pyramid. The base or predictable foundation of the pyramid becomes the letter/sound relationship, so that the reader's single most important task is to develop accurate and speedy sound correspondences for letter patterns. It is assumed that if the reader accomplishes this task effectively the second stage of the pyramid – vocabulary development – will be attained. Printed words will be 'unlockable' through phonics skills. And knowing the words will automatically provide the capstone of *meaning*, completing the reading pyramid (Figure 1).

Figure 1

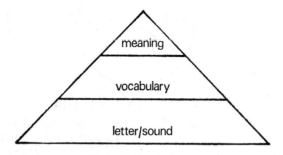

In implementation this model produces instructional materials in which the vocabulary is controlled to present sequenced high-frequency spelling patterns and in which key 'irregular' words are sparingly doled out on a 'need to know' basis. Initial texts using this model contain sequences like the following (Fried, Wilson and Redolph 1966):

A pan is on the van.
A mat is on the van.

Is the fan on the van?
The fan is not on the van.

Is Nat on the van?
Nat is on the van.

When the focus is on controlled spelling patterns, meaning and syntax must be sacrificed.

A second more complex view of reading also perceives it as secondary to oral language but sees the predictable component as being the word. This word-recognition model of reading can be pictured as a pie which is cut into three wedges – one wedge each of letter/sound relationships, word recognition and meaning. While the word-recognition pie shares the same three systems with the phonics pyramid, the placement of the three relates to instructional differences (see Figure 2).

Figure 2

In the pie model the word is seen as being the basic predictable language unit. Letter/sound relationships are treated as one of a number of word recognition skills (i.e. syllabication, derivational and inflectional affixes). It is felt that words are best learned in meaningful sentences and that word recognition skills are best taught on the basis of core sight vocabulary. So the instructional programmes select their vocabulary from lists of commonly-used words, group them as best they can into meaningful contexts, and provide repetitive occurrences to allow for practice. A sample text sequence from such a programme looks like this (Betts and Walch 1963):

Come here, Jimmy and Sue.
Come and look in here.
Look for a toy Jimmy.
And look for a toy, Sue.

When the focus is on vocabulary, syntax and meaning must often be curtailed.

There are two important beliefs concerning language that both the phonics and word-recognition models share. First, they both treat reading as an appendage of speech. Speech is the 'real thing' and reading is speech written down. This is why pronouncing a word aloud is erroneously called decoding in these programmes. Accepting this relationship between speech and reading means that you automatically accept the assumption that reading is more difficult than speaking.

The second belief that they share is that reading is composed of a series of discrete skills and that each of these skills can be isolated for instruction, practised upon, and plugged back into reading. Accepting this principle leads to accepting a dichotomy between 'learning to read' and 'reading to learn'. The learner is asked to put in a long apprenticeship before being declared a reader.

Many people assume that these two views – phonics and word recognition – are the only alternatives available. But there is a third view which can be taken of the reading process. This model of language can be pictured as a golf ball. The core, or heart of the ball, is meaning – the reason for sharing or preserving some thought. This core of meaning is encircled by syntactic structure – the rules for organizing meaning into a shared system. Covering these two inner systems is a surface of sound or of print, so that writing and speech are looked upon as alternative codes for presenting language (see Figure 3).

Each instructional slice which is taken from this model must reach clear to the centre so that it contains all three of the systems operating in their usual language context. This model can be

Figure 3

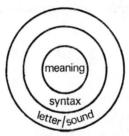

termed a whole-language model. When the focus is upon meaning realized through print, there is no single initial representative text type. The reading materials will vary according to the mode and topic. This model accepts Halliday's notion that using language is 'learning how to mean' and concepts in context become the predictable components of language.

There are three very important beliefs that accompany this whole-language model of reading. First, there is the acceptance that readers are active contributors to the reading process. The one overriding psycholinguistic prerequisite to reading is experience. Reading is an exchange of meanings with an author. While the print is only a code used in the process, reader experience and understanding are the grid through which the author's message is screened. If a reader is not able to draw a relationship between something already known or understood and the author's message, or is uninterested in doing so, reading cannot occur.

Second, readers have to be allowed to make, and to recover from, their own miscues. Reading, like all language, is not exempted from the hypothesizing and testing which is the basis for all other forms of intellectual interaction.

If too high a premium is placed on exact text reproduction, that exactness will be paid for in the reader's inability to attend to meaning. Miscues can result from discrepancies between the author's and the reader's experiences or out of limits on the reader's language strategies. But the same miscues which signal these differences provide processing feedback to the reader.

The third point to be made is that the proficient use of reading strategies develops out of reading experiences. Reading strategies do not have to be developed as the prerequisite to learning to read. All language develops on the basis of need and within meaningful contexts. As Halliday indicates, the functions of language are perceived before the forms of language are produced. In this sense reading instruction should be based on the felt needs of readers, not upon the teacher's anticipation of possible problems.

Clearly, this whole-language model of reading is much more complex than either the phonics or word-recognition models. But this cannot become the argument for rejecting it as the basis for instruction. Complexity cannot be equated with lack of predictability.

While the complexity of the language process might increase the difficulty of the teacher's task – increasing the number of variables which they must take into account in selecting materials and planning instruction – it does not necessarily follow that the user's task is a difficult one.

An analogy can be made between reading and the automobile. The car engine is certainly a complex process – depending for its operation upon the interaction of several systems: electrical, propulsion, exhaust. The automobile mechanic must know the car in terms of the working of its systems. As the systems increase in complexity – as powerbrakes or air conditioners, or dual exhaust is added – the mechanic's job gets harder. The mechanic stands in the same relationship to the automobile as the teacher does to reading instruction. The driver, however, knows the car as a user, interacting with the car as a total process. The very features such as powerbrakes or automatic shift which complicate the mechanic's job actually ease the driver's role. The driver stands in the same relationship to the automobile as the reader does to the text.

Earlier we said that there is only one reading process. While that process is highly complex, it is entirely natural to the social development and interaction of people. The predictability of language is found in its uninterrupted flow within meaningful contexts. *When there is a conflict between what students do naturally and instruction, it is the instruction which must give way.*

References

BETTS, E. and WALCH, C. (1963) 'Time to Play' *Betts Basic Readers* New York: American Book Company

BLOOM, L. (1970) *Language Development* Cambridge, Massachusetts: MIT Press

FRIED, R., WILSON, B. and REDOLPH, S. (1966) Book 1, *Merrill Linguistic Readers* Columbus, Ohio: Charles Merrill Books

HALLIDAY, M. A. K. (1971) *Language Acquisition and Initial Literacy* Claremont Reading Conference, 35th Yearbook; (ed. M. P. Douglass)

2   Towards a professional synthesis

Michael Marland

Unfortunately, most people reckon that they understand what is meant by 'learning to read'. That means that it joins 'discipline', 'large schools', 'spelling', and 'sloppy English' as one of the things about which people worry. Indeed the nation is clearly in an advanced stage of intermittent panic about 'reading'. However, most of the concern, I should suggest, is badly misdirected. The alarmists concentrate on the early years, the initial stages of reading, and the low achievers.

It is not the intensity of this concern that worries me, but its targets. The real problem of reading in our education system comes after the initial stages and concerns pupils more able than the low achievers. The real problems, in fact, are the uses of reading by the older and average or above-average pupil. It is not that they can't read the words, but that they cannot master the sense. However, instead of directing our energies at developing reading skills, study skills, and library-user education, we are trapped by the 'threshold' view of reading: once you are over the threshold, you are out of the cold and there is nothing to worry about. The result of this threshold fallacy is that few middle or secondary schools have anything approaching a whole-school reading approach, far less a 'language across the curriculum' policy.

For all but those few who happily take to reading easily, development of the ability to read requires four simple school strategies:

1   an expectation by all a pupil's teachers of the value of reading for learning
2   a range of suitable materials for reading
3   opportunities for reading

4   tuition in all aspects of reading.

These conditions are no more than what is required in any other part of the curriculum, and are straightforward enough. Yet, I think it can be shown that in most schools there is a serious deficiency in all four respects. There may be some disbelief at such a sweeping statement. After all, when the public are not criticizing teachers for failing to teach children to read, are they not criticizing us for being 'bookish'? But, in fact, I think the majority of pupils are in schools where the following four conditions apply:

1   too many teachers set little value by reading as a way of learning
2   the range of reading materials is frequently (usually?) restricted in quantity and suitability
3   a normal range of lessons offers very few, very short opportunities for reading, and little planning is given to these
4   after the basic stages, and except in literature, there is very, very little tuition at all!

Oddly, a political quirk has confused the issue. Many prominent educators from the left end of the political spectrum have dubbed reading a 'skill', and some even an irrelevant 'middle-class' one at that. It is a curious irony that 'reading standards' became, for a while at least, the public monopoly of right-wing educationists, and this made it harder for those intelligent, committed, and sympathetic teachers flowing into secondary schools in the late 1960s to see the real importance of worrying about reading. The paradox is that if you really want independent learners, you must increase 'teacher-dominated' skills teaching. In fact, all these polarities are misleading, and in the over-politicized 1960s they did indeed mislead: the virtues of 'left-wing' educational ideals depend on a serious concern with reading – at all levels.

The Bullock Report might have marked the end of the old problems and a new start. It seems to me that in the main drift of the argument and in all the mass of detail, the report has four powerful characteristics:

1   it argues against polarities, not to achieve mere surface com-

26

promise, but because the extreme positions on the teaching of language and reading do not stand up to analysis

2 it is interventionist, asking the teacher to find ways of giving specific help at all stages

3 it is a plea for continuity and interrelatedness in all aspects of language teaching, but especially in reading, and this means the continuing of teaching right up the secondary years

4 above all, it implies the need for a synthesis, so that all the professional skills can be brought together to help the pupil.

It is this synthesis that seems to me the greatest need in the profession, and I should have thought that we are now better placed than ever to achieve it – after the Bullock Report, with substantial staff stability, and a new emphasis on in-service training.

I shall discuss this desirable synthesis in two parts, looking mainly at pupils aged eleven years and older: first, *The situation now*; and second, *The possibilities ahead of us*.

The situation now
Four factors come together to create the need for a new professional synthesis:

1 The separateness of specialists
All the influences conspire to keep specialists apart:
(a) the pleasant school tradition of keeping off the patch of others, and the humility of not claiming knowledge one has not got both lead us to leave certain topics to the specialist
(b) the deeply etched departmental separatism, which runs through the whole of education from university and college of education, cuts right into the secondary and middle school
(c) the new influence of industrial management, with its emphasis on the 'line manager', has developed this still further, especially as we have *not* borrowed the even more significant thing about industrial management: frequent compulsory in-service training and shifts of responsibility.

Thus at a meeting of NATE (National Association for the Teaching of English) there are few if any members of UKRA or of NARE (National Association for Remedial Education). At a meeting of SLA (School Library Association) there are even fewer members of any of the three previously mentioned organizations. The teaching of reading is seen as related to remedial work, but not to literature (a very funny split that!); the teaching of library skills (to the extent that it is done at all) is not seen as related to the teaching of reading; linguistics is felt to be alien to literature; fact to fiction; finding out to imagining . . . and so on. I even know an infant school which sets out the divisions in the youngest years by dividing its book stock into 'work books' and 'reading books'!

Particularly sad is the isolation of much 'remedial' work and many 'remedial' teachers. Their syllabuses are often not concordant with the main syllabuses of the school; their interests are only with those who are slow learners, and rarely do they find out about the reading difficulties of average or above-average pupils. Even more rarely would a British school consider trying to develop their expertise in helping the brighter pupil develop his reading skills further. And as for the library – frequently pupils getting 'remedial' help in a school have even less help in understanding library and study skills than the other pupils.

The librarian, whether chartered professional librarian or teacher-librarian, is often kept in a separate world: never consulted about syllabus planning; frequently not even informed of major curriculum changes; having to wheedle for copies of departmental syllabuses; and getting reading lists only for sixth-formers. It is rumoured that one member of the School Library Association asked at a committee meeting what point there was in giving evidence to the Bullock Committee as it was a committee on *reading*! Certainly, few professional librarians have had much opportunity to learn about learning to read. Recent shifts in resource-based learning have sadly made this aspect worse by pushing the librarian towards the audio-visual aids department and even further away from the reading specialist. The librarian trainers and writers who are interested in reading tend to specialize in children's fiction – important certainly, but not the whole of reading.

Of course, apart from librarians, linguists, remedial teachers, English teachers and reading specialists, there is another group: the subject specialists. Their isolation from the other groups is well understood, and Bullock pleads against it. However, the gap remains stubbornly intractable. Language, says the subject specialist, is merely something we *use*: let others develop it. As for reading, that is a skill pupils should have got under their belts in junior schools.

This disparity of specialists does not constitute a set of groups at war with each other, but groups kept apart by history, training, career structure, school organization – and, I believe, by having too much respect for the mysteries of each other's craft.

2 *The conspiracy against print*

Such a dramatic phrase may not appear appropriate for any educational problem, but the phenomenon I have in mind warrants the most alarmist terms, and sometimes seems like a conspiracy.

Word has got around that 'textbooks are too difficult', and certainly pupils do have considerable difficulty getting much understanding from books in lessons. At first glance this seems to support the thesis. The other possible part of the reason why pupils are not helped to understand print as a learning source is less often considered. Hearing that modern analysis confirms one's worst fears, encourages the teachers to use fewer books, to use them less often, and not to think carefully about how to use them.

For all its faults, the now much-derided textbook is an ideal individualized reading scheme: the pupil can reread the Science chapter for homework; he can read ahead in the Geography book; he can even pick bits out from the History book. By comparison many of the worksheet or card schemes dole out tiny portions of print and the pupil can read only those dollops and only at the permitted time. (It is a curious irony that the more teacher-directed card and worksheet are seen as 'child-centred' and 'left-wing', whilst the book, which in fact gives the pupil greater freedom, is often seen as 'teacher-centred' and 'right-wing'.)

Not only do many of the schemes in use involve less reading, but the teacher circumnavigates what is there! The Mathematics teacher explains in his own words what is perfectly well explained in the book; the craft teacher hands out cards with instructions, and then explains exactly what to do. Just about all of us, when a pupil asks about a word or a sentence, *tell* him, without helping him to deduce it from the context! Rarely do we help the pupil to get through the text; often do we help him to get *round* it.

Such approaches are common, especially in the more conscientious teacher, who is so determined to work hard to help the pupil to understand that he helps the pupil to *avoid* the reading problem. This not only eliminates a reading opportunity, but gives the message through the hidden curriculum that reading is an unnecessary difficulty to be avoided if possible.

3   The dearth of non-narrative

There is an alarming anomaly within the reading curriculum throughout the adolescent years: reading tuition is given in two ways only – the basic skills to the slow or backward learner, and literature skills to the rest. Thus the bulk of the reading experience and teaching for most pupils is with literature, especially narrative. However, the bulk of reading for learning – in subject textbooks and library 'research' projects – is with non-narrative. As the Bullock Report commented, this teaching is normally of a very high standard, and the literary response evoked in school after school is very impressive. Perhaps in the pre-O-level year, the looming memory of the précis turns the pupils to non-narrative, but it would probably be fair to say that nine-tenths of the reading experience in which any help is given is narrative. I have already spoken of the reduced quantity of reading in subjects other than English. What is further remarkable is how little help is given to older pupils when their studies do require reading. The Science teacher who carefully prepares for the use of any new piece of apparatus, and who gives detailed advice during its use, thinks nothing of flinging out brief instructions to read a chapter of a textbook without any advice, guidance or preparation. It is no wonder that teachers of older pupils find that their pupils have great difficulty with their reading.

I do not have to point out the differences between narrative and non-narrative prose – differences which require very different techniques. It is worth pointing out, though, that all of the English lessons favour narrative. For instance, word-building and etymology, aids to understanding the vocabulary of non-narrative, are little taught. The relationship of the teaching of spelling to word structure and meaning has been little exploited in the classroom. Furthermore, the work that is done on vocabulary throughout the years of schooling concentrates on the vocabulary of narrative: nouns, adjectives, verbs, adverbs. Rarely if ever are the *Head of Department* Heinemann Educational Books (1971) chapter will discuss 'stumble' but not 'since' or 'nevertheless'.

There is a similar mismatch between the teaching of punctuation in the classroom and what is needed by the reader of non-narrative. There is a concentration particularly on punctuation for writing, with little or no work on *reading* punctuation, and the narrative/non-narrative balance is still kept in favour of the first. Compare, for instance, the efforts we put into teaching the use of paragraph indentation and quotation marks for story dialogue with the considerably less time given to commas. Actually, we almost completely lack a way of explaining commas, semi-colons and full stops.

I should thus argue that the pupil is ill prepared by the language and reading experience and tuition in most schools even for the reading diet that will be offered in the year or so before the end of statutory schooling. Very odd curriculum planning!

4   Whatever happened to language across the curriculum?
The massive recommendations of the Bullock Committee have become encapsulated in the phrase 'language across the curriculum'. This is the actual wording in the context of secondary education:

138   In the secondary school, all subject teachers need to be aware of:
(i)   the linguistic processes by which their pupils acquire information and understanding, and the implications for the teacher's own use of language;
(ii)   the reading demands of their own subjects, and ways in which the pupils can be helped to meet them.
139   To bring about this understanding every secondary school should develop a policy for language across the curriculum. The responsibility for this policy should be embodied in the organizational structure of the school.

Precisely because of the separatist factors that I have mentioned, this essentially synthesizing ambition has been unscrambled too often whilst schools have actually been working on the policy.

The effort of linking language with curriculum has been so daunting for most schools that many have almost unconsciously shed some of the components. One of those most often shed has been reading. As a result, many schools moving towards a language policy have been concerned substantially with writing, or, in the more fashionable schools, talking.

Whereas the Schools Council's *Writing Across the Curriculum* Project has been extremely effective in reaching many teachers of English, and not a few other subject teachers, the work on reading has remained inside UKRA, and has been taken up primarily by those working with the younger or less able pupils. Whereas there has been felt to be something challenging and 'progressive' about the Bullock Report's recommendations on, say, the place of talk in learning, its recommendations on reading have been more complex and required closer study. For one reason or another there has been no equivalent of Nancy Martin on writing or Douglas Barnes on talking to capture the paperback-reading teacher's imagination. This 'reading stuff' is less amenable to exciting seminar chat, and is more like hard pedagogical work.

Another aspect of this is the political structure of schools. I see it as very unfortunate that 'language across the curriculum' has usually been seen as the English department's responsibility. It should, of course, be seen as a *curriculum* matter, and therefore more relevant to the Deputy in charge of the curriculum than to the Head of English. It is vital now to get it out of the hands of English specialists. For one thing, the specialist secondary Head of English is usually exclusively literature trained, and feels ill at ease and pretty ignorant when faced with the requirements of the Bullock Report's demands for a language and reading policy. These demands seem to undermine his position in the school by revealing his ignorance, whereas it at least appears that the talking and writing recommendations are right up his street. They strengthen his position by seeming to show his classroom styles as more ideal than those of his other subject colleagues.

The possibilities ahead of us

But there is definite hope. From one point of view the Bullock Report can be seen as the great unifying document, showing schools the need for coherent planning [I develop my idea of the coherent school in *Comprehensive Schools* Heinemann Educational Books, forthcoming], and showing the professions the way to work together (although the Report was arguably at its weakest on libraries, seeing the problem too simply in terms of financial provision, and insufficiently in terms of teaching). I see ahead of us the need to create a new professional synthesis.

1 A shared professionalism

When from time to time we reject the separatism of our different specialisms, there are two directions to which people usually turn; the first is to a nostalgic memory of the 'general subjects' teachers of the elementary school and the secondary modern school; the second is to 'integration', which joins two or three existing subjects into a more or less cohesive single entity. Whatever the merits on other grounds of either solution, neither solves the problem I described in the first part. The first denies specialism and keeps it away from the education of pupils; the second masks the separatism by creating a few major blocks. However, it is not a jot easier for a librarian to penetrate half a dozen faculty blocks of integrated subjects than it is for him to influence the older separate subjects; indeed it may be harder. Similarly, most of the integrated faculty blocks will still be without any reading expertise, and there is no certainty that it will be easier for them to acquire it.

What I look to is something more difficult: I should like to see each of the specialists in a school developing that specialism very sharply indeed, and I should like to see the school as a whole relishing the otherness of each specialism. After all, librarians and reading specialists, mathematicians and junior teachers, remedial teachers and science teachers have different drives, have been trained differently, and spend their working week with different primary concerns. These differences should not be smoothed away by asking everyone to do the same thing in the same proportion. Instead we need to find ways of using and exploiting these specialisms.

The function of a specialist in a team is twofold. Arguably the least important part is the day-to-day work in that specialism, even though it uses most of the person's time. *More important is making the specialism available to assist the work of others.* (I have described this method of building up a departmental team in *Head of Department* Heinemann Educational Books (1971) chapter 2 'The Complementary Team'.) Thus a school can be seen as a team of varied specialists, and the task of management in a school is to find ways of enabling the team as a whole to make use of the specialisms of each. This means considering the needs of the pupils, finding out who knows what, and setting up schemes for making this knowledge available to the other teachers.

One of the marvellous things about working in a school staff is that there is usually someone who knows about anything you need to know about. We must learn to learn from each other. In the field we are considering, this means generalizing from the knowledge of the librarian, the remedial teacher, the English teacher, the subject specialist, and the reading expert. It also frequently means looking to the infant and junior teacher.

2 School-focused in-service training

The two cardinal advantages of school-focused in-service training from this point of view are that it is generated by a school to meet its own needs, and, secondly, that the best use can be made of the talents and skills within a staff. It is, indeed, a synthesizing process and focuses the synthesis on the school staff as a group, thus helping to bring together their problems and their skills.

There are sometimes misunderstandings about the phrase 'school-focused in-service training'. It does not indicate the location, the contributors, or even the organizers. It declares that the school as a client group has articulated its own need, and it is that need for this particular group of professionals that is to be met. The work can be organized by an outsider, such as the local adviser or a Department of Education lecturer, but even so the courses are tailor-made for the particular school, and may use both outside experts and members of the school staff as contributors.

The problems of developing reading for learning are much easier to discuss in the context of particular sequences of lessons and particular pupils and teachers. They involve three stages:

1 planning the uses of print in learning
2 analysing the difficulties that pupils have

3   devising teaching strategies.

In considering these points, the teacher of English is not necessarily, nor indeed even normally, the best placed to advise. He or
she often has no particular experience or expertise in the first two,
and only a little in the third. Similarly, the remedial expert will
have some contributions to make to help all his colleagues, but
will not often have a great deal of experience beyond the basic
stages of reading. The librarian will also have something to offer.
Lucky the school that has a reading specialist, perhaps having
done an OU course, in one of the subject departments other than
English.

A one-day closure followed by a sequence of seminars, can be
based on the actual reading problems encountered in the school.
Perhaps the starting point would be a collection of passages from
texts that are used in classes, and a consideration of actual research
assignments set by teachers.

One of the most practical steps the United Kingdom Reading
Association could take would be to devise material precisely for
use in school-focused in-service training. There is a real need for
translating the knowledge about intermediate and higher reading
skills into a form that can be used in staff seminars.

3   Whole-school curriculum planning
Virtually all curriculum planning that goes on in schools is unit
planning; that is, consideration is given to one component at a
time. The Geography syllabus for the last two years of compulsory schooling is exchanged for the Schools Council's *Geography
for the Young School Leaver*; the Mathematics department goes over
to a new course book; the Science department integrates Physics,
Biology and Chemistry for the younger pupils; and so on. Very
few Heads of Department meetings discuss the *whole* curriculum,
except in timetable or option terms; there is very little knowledge
in one department of the other; however much vertical consultation there may be, there is virtually no horizontal consultation.

This unit approach is inimical to any 'across the curriculum'
attempt. Indeed, I have come to feel that the difficulty about
implementing 'language across the curriculum' is that most of us
have no curriculum across which to put it. The unit approach has

to find a unit into which 'reading' will go – and 'English' seems the most likely slot. 'Reading' thus becomes one unit and not a skill needed by and taught in all units. What is more, the reading experience is devised only with the needs of subject English in mind.

What I find encouraging is that schools that do have a central planning mechanism find it fairly easy to consider the Bullock Committee's plea for a 'language across the curriculum' policy. Of course, there are still difficulties of implementation, but there is no serious difficulty in seeing what it is about and how to start on it. Perhaps even more encouraging, other schools are finding in the Bullock Report the means of producing a whole-school planning mechanism. The Report can be seen as both demanding and assisting a coherent approach to school curriculum planning.

A whole-school approach to the curriculum asks the staff of a school to consider what learning experiences are considered desirable, and then to discuss who teaches these, when, and how. Such an approach analyses the requirements of each aspect of the learning experience, and plans how to facilitate it (not necessarily leaving every department to help itself alone). Such a consideration is likely to demand a whole-school reading syllabus, linked to study skills and library use; both taught specifically, and used and reinforced by all teachers who use print.

Any consideration of the curriculum inevitably involves a consideration of the uses of reading beyond the basic skills. There is no hope of 'getting reading right' without looking at the whole curriculum of pupils aged eleven years and older. With the gradual growth of whole-school curriculum planning, though, there is a growing hope that reading will take its proper place – be used and taught.

4 School liaison

Much is piously said about liaison between schools, but it is usually remarkably general and vague. Most liaison achievements are pastoral rather than concerned with the curriculum, and most arrangements depend too heavily on the goodwill and personal relationships of individuals.

The Bullock Report joined the queue of official exhortations to teachers to produce the almost mystical liaison, but it rooted the plea in sharp practicalities. Page 77 is headed by that powerful quotation from I. A. Richards, 'We are all of us learning to read all our lives'. The corollary of that, of course, is that we teachers are all of us expected to help young people with their learning to read throughout all their school lives. This not only suggests liaison, it suggests a coherent syllabus from the age of five to sixteen plus.

Thus, the Bullock Report translates the vague concept of 'liaison' from the realms of mere good relationships into a scheme for action, which is another perspective of the professional synthesis for which I am calling. The scheme requires:

(a) knowledge of teaching methods across the institutional divides

(b) knowledge and planning of reading material used

(c) an agreed policy on standardized tests and the passing on of suitable objectively measured information about pupils

(d) the passing on of examples of a pupil's writing in various modes from one school to another.

Obviously, the latter two are easier to achieve than the former two, for they imply actual agreement on teaching method! From small details like the name for: " " (do we call them 'sixty-six and ninety-nine', or 'speech marks', or 'inverted commas', or 'quotation marks'?), through to major matters like teaching strategies for the higher reading skills, the Bullock Report implies the need for shared planning of the curriculum and of the teaching methods.

I have been encouraged by the number of areas where a 'community of schools' have come together to create this kind of planning. It is highly beneficial to the teachers concerned to learn from each other in the process of planning. It is, incidentally, surely the only way in which the autonomy of the schools can be preserved, for if we cannot devise a language and reading curriculum for ourselves, are we not asking for a centrally - or LEA - imposed curriculum?

5 Study skills

In moments of idealism, we often speak of our aims of independent learning, continuing education, and the value of critical thought. We set 'investigatory homeworks', and CSE candidates are engaged in 'research projects'. How carefully, though, do we teach the necessary skills? In the past, rather infrequently and very inadequately.

I sense that there is a new spirit abroad. A few schools are actually working out what is required for activities as small as an apparently simple piece of looking up ('For homework, find out what you can about bilharzia' – an example of so many Humanities or Science homework assignments), to major undertakings such as the CSE projects demanded by very many subjects. Such a working out produces a sequence that starts with the tasks of focusing, survey and accessing; then goes on to the skills of extended non-narrative reading; and finally involves skills of extraction, selection, writing up, and reorganization. Perhaps the British Library's research project on Library-User Education in Secondary Schools (directed by Ann Irving) is a sign that we have entered a new era of real attempts to find out what needs to be done to help the student. As a US federal study of the problem declares: 'A librarian is a teacher whose subject is learning itself.' That, however, is not yet a definition that British librarians would apply to themselves or which British teachers would apply to their librarian colleagues.

I should see one of the results of the synthesis for which I am calling in the production within a 'community of schools' of a study-skills and library-use syllabus from five to sixteen years, a true 'spiral curriculum' in which the same problems are explored at different levels of complexity in each year. Such a syllabus, both its drawing-up and teaching, will, however, demand a collaborative approach, for no one specialist has all the necessary knowledge or experience.

6 Language across the curriculum

Finally, and despite the fears and criticisms I have expressed, the impetus of the Bullock Committee's recommendations are still growing in force as LEAs, groups of schools, and individual schools study the recommendations in the light of their own needs and experience. The Committee did not spell out the details, although most of them are in the Report. (I have detailed my own views on what such a policy should be and how it should be implemented in Language Across the Curriculum Heinemann

Educational Books 1977.) To create a policy requires the specialists to come together to contribute to a common learning approach. This certainly encourages the professional synthesis for which I plead.

Conclusion

I sometimes despairingly see the middle and secondary schools as elaborate organizations for increasing the language differentials between pupils: those who come in weak in language but not bad enough for remedial work are given fewer language-based tasks; those who are weaker at reading are provided, in much modern mixed-ability teaching, with tasks requiring less and easier reading; at option time these pupils choose more of the non-reading subjects; as considerable efforts are made by their teachers to simplify the reading and reduce its length and the number of occasions on which it is necessary, little thought or effort is put into helping the pupil with what reading tasks remain.

Yet much learning is by reading, and the highest ideals of encouraging independent study are heavily reliant on reading ability. If we are to come near to achieving these aims, we must plan the reading experiences and reading tuition throughout the school years, both as an essential part of the curriculum and as an essential way of helping other parts of the curriculum. Such a task cannot be seen as the prerogative of the teachers of English. It requires us all to pull together in a new professional synthesis.

Part 2

Learning to read

Learning to read

Introduction

To divide the field of reading into a 'learning to read' area and a 'reading to learn' area is useful, because it helps to focus attention on two extremely important aspects of the whole field. The dichotomy is, however, a bit artificial, since 'learning to read' is – or at least should be – a long-term developmental process and not confined to two or three years of infant schooling.

This section concentrates on a limited number of fundamental aspects of beginning reading. The five contributors do not have identical views of the nature of reading and of learning to read. But they do have something very important in common: all of them see reading as something much more than 'barking at print', more than 'decoding' black marks on paper and translating them into speech. They see reading as integrated in the wider area of language and communication, as a purposeful activity that can never be reduced to technicalities. This does not mean that they want to ignore the 'technical' *aspects* of reading; they just want to place these aspects in a wider context.

The section starts with Moira McKenzie's plea for reading as the major means of learning to read. To those used to a step-by-step analysing and synthesizing approach, with progress from letter-sound to syllable to word and so on, this may seem like a paradox, since children cannot 'read' until they have 'learned to read'. But the whole idea seems much more acceptable if we can assume that 'reading' is a question of degree – of *how much meaning* is picked up by the individual reader. The goal remains the same – good reading that results in the richest possible communication between writer and reader – although the way to get there may be new.

Geoff Roberts argues for a reappraisal of the teaching of reading with less emphasis on analysis and abstraction – in which infants are weak – and more emphasis on communication of meaningful language – in which they are much stronger. The reading programme he proposes is meant to be part of an integrated language programme, so that, in his own words, 'reading no longer stands apart as an isolated skill'.

The need for a programme or a plan is underlined by Bridie Raban, too, who discusses the organizing of materials and other resources for individual pupil progress in reading. She underlines the need for a 'master-plan' that guides the progress of the beginner, but she also emphasizes that the plan must be adjusted in each case so that it suits the individual child. It is worth pointing out, in our opinion, that a planned, systematic approach is quite compatible with the notion that children learn to read mainly through reading.

Equal opportunity does not mean that all children are given the same teaching, argues Larry Carrillo, who borrows some of his arguments from Shakespeare's *Hamlet*. Equal opportunity means that all children have an equal chance to learn what they are ready to learn, when they are ready. And it means that teachers should help those who are not yet ready, so that they become ready. We may not all agree about when it is 'ideal' to start 'formal' teaching of reading, and Larry Carrillo certainly does not pretend to have the final answer. But careful assessment of the potentials and needs of each child is surely required in order to provide a solid foundation for later reading development.

Finally, Betty Coody's paper reminds us of the importance of literature in the education of young children. The evaluation of books for children is largely a question of subjective judgment, and whether or not one values a particular genre of books will depend, among other things, on how one views the purposes of reading and the uses of literature in school. We do believe, though, that there can be no disagreement about the need for a varied and well-balanced library for young children.

3 Learning to read through reading

Moira McKenzie

Many youngsters have been introduced to literacy at home. They've shared books with a loved adult. They know stories. They have favourite books. In a literate society children meet written language in the names of shops, road signs, TV adverts, and favourite cereals, both on the breakfast table and on the supermarket shelves. They have met written language in imaginative and functional and practical forms; thus they already have some knowledge of purpose for reading, and the satisfaction to be found in enjoyment of books and stories.

Such knowledge seems to be basic to learning to read. There is evidence (Clark 1976; Downing 1977) that youngsters with such experience are the ones most able to cope with the sort of teaching they often meet in school. The ones at greatest risk are those whose first awareness of literacy occurs in school. For, in an overconcern for reading to be learned quickly, teachers tend to emphasize decoding skills. This gives the uninitiated a very narrow and restricted view of what reading is and what it means to be literate, a view that may well dog them throughout their school days and hamper further learning.

Two requirements in learning to read
Learning to read requires getting to understand both the communicative function of written language, and its technical features (Clark 1976; Downing 1977). The former is concerned with purpose and message; the latter with understanding the system; that is, knowing how written language works. These two aspects are integral. The beginning reader can, while working within the communicative element of reading and writing, learn the technical features, and gradually acquire the skills that will enable him to use written language independently. The teacher plays a vital role

45

Table 1 Approximating to text: 'A Fairy Story'

Barbara 5.8 Text	1st reading (14 Nov.)	2nd reading (17 Nov., a.m.)	3rd reading (17 Nov., p.m.)
P.1 Once upon a time there was a poor boy.	Once upon a time there lived . . . Once *apon* a time lived a boy and he had no mummies and no daddy and no clothes.	Once upon a time there lived a poor boy.	Once upon . . . Once upon a time there lived a poor boy.
P.2 he didn't have a coat.	He walked in and out of the people but he did not find a mummy.	He had no coat. „ „ „ „	He had not coat.
P.3 he didn't have a home or a bed.	He lied on the grass. He had no bed.	and no house and no bed.	and he had no bed or no clothes.
P.4 he didn't go to school.	And one day he saw the school people and he followed them.	He had no school. He had no house.	He never went to school.
P.5 he didn't watch television.		He never watched telly. „ „ „	
P.6 he didn't play with toys.	And he had no clothes, no money or no bed.	He had no toys.	He didn't have any clothes.
P.7 he didn't have a friend.	he didn't have any friend.	He didn't have any friends.	He didn't have any friends.

in highlighting appropriate technical features within a context of meaning.

The question in respect to teaching reading is not centred about 'code emphasis' or 'meaning emphasis' but rather on the role of each of them as children learn to read. Two critical elements are involved: the powerful role of the child's intention to get at meaning and his urge to gain control over what he does, and the nature of reading skills.

Reading for meaning: the communicative function

From the beginning, reading 'skills' include more complex language and thinking processes than simply decoding symbol to sound. The knowledgeable teacher expects the young reader from whatever linguistic or experience background to use his knowledge and language/thinking skills to get to the meaning of the text. She enables him to engage in continuing dialogue with the text, to respond to it, to take on the message or story and make it his own. As Margaret Clark (1976) states: 'The teacher who regards teaching as a communication skill will use a very different approach from the teacher for whom reading is decoding into spoken language.' (p. 5)

In Table 1 we see the responses of Barbara, a beginning reader aged 5·8 to *A Fairy Story*. We can see how her language and experience interact with the text as she 'reads' the story to her teacher on three successive occasions.

This story was one of many to be found in the book corner. The teacher (one of an ongoing course at CLPE) read it to Barbara and then invited her to 'read' it. She tape-recorded the child 'reading' it. Barbara could return to the book as often as she liked, take it home to 'read', share it with a friend in the book corner. The teacher, however, read it to Barbara and tape-recorded her 'reading' it on two more occasions. She transcribed it in the way shown above as a way of monitoring the 'reading'. She wanted to study Barbara's response to the story and her understanding of it. She wanted to examine her language in the first reading and her further shift towards the language of the text. At the same time, she wished to observe closely how Barbara handled the book, how she was progressing towards the concept of directionality, and the attention she paid to the print itself.

As we examine the text we can see that Barbara is obviously processing the story. She uses the book as a reader does, going through the story page by page, 'reading' it as best she can, drawing upon her own experience, using her own and the author's language to reconstruct the story she has had read to her.

When we examine the transcript, we observe a big difference between the first and second reading. In the first we can see clearly how Barbara uses her own language and experience in reproducing the story; for example, 'he had no mummies and no daddy and no clothes'. This is a summary statement of Barbara's that reflects her concept of a poor boy. Nowhere in the text itself does it say explicitly that the poor boy had no parents. She also 'reads': 'he walked in and out of the people but he didn't find a mummy', again using her own experience to elaborate upon the text, plus information from the accompanying picture. She infers a causal connection between the picture cues and the written text when she 'reads': 'He lied on the grass. He had no bed.'

Barbara has 'taken on' this story in her own way and gone beyond the actual words in the text to produce an oral text that is an integration of her language and experience with that provided in the story. In the second and third 'readings' she is much closer to the text itself. She is still reconstructing the text, not just reciting it by heart. She gradually revises her language to conform to the text. When she is at the stage where she is able to read the words actually written on the page, i.e. the surface structure of language, Barbara brings her personal meanings and images to construing the text. Her performance is consistent with Frederiksen's (1975) observations about people's ability to recall texts they have heard or read. He showed how individual, personal knowledge influences the way a text is remembered: 'As the subject builds up a semantic structure for a text, the derived information becomes an integral part of the subject's understanding of the text.' (p. 168) He says further that in his studies he has found evidence that the derived material, in Barbara's case her elaborations and inferences, is maintained as part of the reader's knowledge structure when the reader checks his memory of the text against the text itself.

Becoming aware of features of written language

Arguments put forward in the Bullock Report, and by scholars such as Barnes (1971, 1976), the Rosens (1973) and Britton (1970), demonstrate the need for learners to use their own language in assimilating new learning, and to organize and reorder their present knowledge. Could such arguments be applied to the way children need to learn to read, and to learn how the written system operates? We can see how Barbara, given the opportunity to behave as a reader, responds to the story and gets to know about reading even before she can read.

It was apparent from observing her behaviour throughout the three readings that she is learning some essential features of written language, such as:

the text carries the message;
a book is read from left to right, page by page;
the amount of language spoken is related to the amount of print on the page.

Similar understandings of written language are generated in the language-experience activities used by many teachers as they help youngsters create and use reading material that relate to their own experiences, expressed in their own language. Both are instances of communication in which the child gets the chance to see written language as representative of his own meanings (Halliday 1971). The opportunity to hear and read stories goes further, for it extends the child's own language and allows him to take on story structure, and written-language structures in his own way. This holds true for all children, whatever their linguistic background. It is particularly valuable for non-standard and second-language speakers as we see in the following two examples – the first from a child in South East London; the second, a boy from Bangladesh in a North London school.

This example shows Michelle, aged 5·6, 'reading' the story *Titch*, coping with comparative language structures.

Text	*Response*
Titch was little.	Titch was very small.
His sister Mary was a bit bigger.	Titch's sister was a bit more bigger.

Text	Response
And his brother Pete was a lot bigger.	And Pete was very very big.
Pete had a great big bike.	Pete had the biggest bike.
Mary had a big bike.	Mary had a big bike.
And Titch had a little tricycle.	And Titch had a little . . . [teacher:] tricycle.

The next example shows Mammun, aged 7, learning English as a second language.

Text	Response
Titch was little.	Titch is little.
His sister Mary was a bit bigger.	His sister Mary was bit much bigger.
And his brother Pete was a lot bigger.	His brother Peter was more bigger.
Pete had a great big bike.	Peter had big big bike.
And Titch had a little tricycle.	And Titch was little tiny bike.

At the end of the story Mammun provides this interesting example of his present understanding of past tense in English:

And Titch's seed grew	it growed
and grew	it growed
and grew.	it growed high.

He seems to have internalized the rule for forming the past tense by adding *ed*, but has not yet sorted out the exceptions. Where the text read: 'Pete had a big spade', Mammun responded: 'Peter had . . .' and then paused for a long time, looking at the picture: '. . . big dig!' The word spade was not yet in his English vocabulary. It was evident as one listened to Mammun, and studied his transcript, that he understood the story, and that he was using and extending his growing knowledge of English to construct his own meanings. If the language that carries the meaning is new, or if the child is working on particular concepts or ideas, he will need to hear the text again and again before he can easily take on the language of the text. As he reads and constructs his own meanings, he is helped to accommodate to the visual constraints of the print, to repeated patterns, eventually recognizing a one-to-one correspondence between the word he says and the form he sees.

Teachers enable children to behave as readers in the ways described because they give them access to the text, either because the story (book) has been read to them – and with them – or because they have created the text together. They are given what Morris (1973) calls one-hundred-per-cent context support. Since the child at this stage is not yet a reader he has to be helped into any text in some way. A common way is to use a book with a limited and tightly controlled vocabulary, and through the use of flash-cards and word games teach the child to recognize the words he will meet in the book. The misconception is that, when he meets these known words in the text, he will not only be able to identify them but to generate meaning from them. But since such texts often lack meaning, rarely have any kind of story line, and often use unnatural, contrived language, a series of obstacles are immediately put in his path. There is no way children can see such language as representative of any kind of meaning they understand. Hence, we begin teaching reading, a complex process involving the reader in active response, employing cues from many sources, especially language, as if reading were concerned only with word recognition.

The teacher using language and story experience operates from a different understanding of reading. She can offer the child better reading material, real stories, because she anticipates that he will work on the text to get at the meaning in his own way. She does not expect him to begin by getting all the words right. The stories he is asked to tackle provide motivation and satisfaction on his own terms. Because they have a very clear story structure and appropriate language which, although simple, is real language, these stories are actually easier to read than the 'primerese' of many beginning-reading books. The learner begins reading with an expectation that it will make sense and sound like the language of stories. From the beginning he engages in dialogue about what he is reading; he actively processes the text, responds to it, increasingly draws closer to the author's language, and gradually gets to know about the visual aspects of print.

The technical aspects of reading

Thus, the communicative aspect of reading is assured, but what about the technical features to be learned? As the child 'reads', the teacher positively helps him acquire appropriate skills of dealing with graphic and phonic features of language. Marie Clay (1973) calls this stage 'emergent reading'. As the child 'reads', the teacher helps him learn directional rules. She asks, 'Where shall I read now?' She finds out how he's organizing his reading by suggesting that he points as he reads, where it is appropriate. She helps him discern significant features of words and letters as she makes comments such as:

> Here's that word *Mary* again. It begins the same as your name. Can you hear it? Mm-Mary. Mm-Michelle.
> Yes. It's a little word like *is* – but it's *in*. How is it different?
> I thought you put it there because it has the same pattern at the end (referring to words like *doing* and *scribbling*).

The teacher invites the child to reflect upon his own reading behaviour and conjecture about particular features. She asks:

> How did you know it was *Titch*?
> How did you know it wasn't *is*?

She further helps the young reader get to know and be explicit about specific phonic knowledge as he needs to use it in his early attempts at writing. Gradually, she helps the young reader know *how* to look and *what* to look for, to be discriminating about features of print, not just try to remember them. She encourages him to predict and learn how to check his predictions against a range of language and visual cues. She helps him develop the language needed to talk about language, e.g. word, letter, sentence, etc. She is concerned that he should recognize that written language is a language system. She is aware that 'cognitive clarity' (Vernon 1957) comes with understanding and using the system.

So, the two aspects of learning to read, *viz.* understanding both its communicative function and its technical features, remain integral. Skills are taught and learned in the process of the larger meaningful act of getting meaning from written language. Global response gives way to more precise reading of the text. Predictions are checked against language and phonic knowledge. For reading skills include using a whole range of language and thinking features as well as the simple decoding skills that so often distort early reading instruction.

References

BARNES, D. (1971) (revised edition) *Language, the Learner and the School* Penguin

BARNES, D. (1976) *From Communication to Curriculum* Penguin

BREAKTHROUGH BOOKS (1973) *A Fairy Story* Yellow Set E. Longman

BRITTON, J. (1970) *Language and Learning* Pelican

CLARK, M. (1976) *Young Fluent Readers* Heinemann Educational

CLAY, M. M. (1973) *Reading: the Patterning of Complex Behaviour* Heinemann

DOWNING, J. (1977) *Learning to Read with Understanding* Paper presented at the Annual Convention of the International Reading Association, Miami Beach, Florida, May

FREDERIKSEN, C. K. (1975) Acquisition of semantic information from discourse: effects of repeated exposures *Journal of Verbal Learning and Verbal Behavior* 14, 158–69

HALLIDAY, M. A. K. (1971) *Language Acquisition and Initial Literacy* Claremont Reading Conference, 35th Yearbook; (ed. M. P. Douglass)

HUTCHINS, P. (1972) *Titch* Bodley Head

MORRIS, R. (1973) *Success and Failure in Learning to Read* (New edn with introduction by David Mackay) Penguin

ROSEN, C. and H. (1973) *The Language of Primary School Children* Penguin

VERNON, M. D. (1957) *Backwardness in Reading* Cambridge University Press

4 Time to change: a reappraisal of the teaching of reading

Geoffrey R. Roberts

In this paper it is not the intention to dispute the fact that the majority of children are taught to read in primary schools. Yet the question remains, are teachers using techniques which significantly help the learner or do these techniques leave an undue burden upon him?

Obviously much of the teaching is very good, but it could well be that the current methodological approaches tend to inhibit that teaching and prevent it from achieving the optimum effects in both the short and the long term.

The limitations of decoding

Rereading Huey (1908) recently, the writer found it difficult to disagree with the comment by Kolers in his introduction to the latest reprint of Huey's book that, 'Remarkably little empirical information has been added to what Huey knew', in 1908! There have been developments since Huey wrote, but almost all have begun with the major and virtually exclusive premise that reading is the phonic decoding of words, and hence, there has been no fundamental shift in methodology apart from tentative moves towards a language–experience approach: tentative because in most cases this approach is used only for a minimal period and seldom takes the reader as far as reading texts other than those which he has produced himself. Even look-and-say methods as described by Schonell were basically a word-by-word decoding approach to the interpretation of print. They only differed from a phonic approach in that they required the young learner to rely upon his memory for some nebulous features of words rather than his memory for features illuminated by the teacher. There was little, if any, training in the interpretation of prose. The child simply had to remember words and it was then hoped that he would be able to fit them into a language context himself. Of course the decoding of words is an important part of learning to read; nevertheless, it is not the only, nor is it the major, factor. There are other factors connected with the complexity of language, with the limitations of the learner and with the ways in which teachers organize the children for learning, which deserve serious consideration when planning the learning sequences which will produce an effective and eager reader.

The popular view of reading based almost entirely on the ability to decode individual words, as opposed to the interpretation of words in their total context, is exemplified in the actions of those teachers who, when a child falters over a word whilst reading aloud, suggest that he should 'sound out' that word. This technique makes two assumptions. One is that all words can be derived by the unskilled reader from phonic cues alone, which is patently untrue; consider such common words as *he, that, they, with, come, like, said.* The other assumption is that, at any particular point of failure in reading a passage, all the necessary cues other than phonic cues precede the word, and that what follows does not contribute to word identification. Again this is not true. The word *tears* can only be correctly identified in the sentence, *The girl had tears in her* . . ., by reading beyond it and using semantic cues in addition to phonological–graphemic cues. Furthermore, in order to distinguish between the meanings of *Peter hits Jane* and *Jane hits Peter*, the reader must use the cues provided by the position of the words.

The only conclusion that can be drawn from these three examples is that the reader must use a multi-cue approach and that training is necessary. He must accept the fact that he cannot rely solely upon one set of cues. This fact is emphasized when one considers that a high proportion of the words in the early books of most reading schemes are irregular, and therefore cannot be 'discovered' by using phonic cues alone. Hence the young unskilled reader must rely upon the text or his memory to give him the necessary information that he requires. But the texts of all the early reading books are so loose that informed guessing and anticipation are impossible. (Most of these books consist of staccato sentences, each a discrete statement which is rarely linked together in meaning with the other sentences on the page. A randomly selected sequence from a well-known set of reading books will illustrate this point: *Here is Nip. Dick has the dog. I see Nip and Jane.*) Hence the child is unable to use all the cues at his command, and he has to rely almost entirely upon his memory for phonic cues and words – an ability in which he has severe limitations.

Rationale for a new methodology

Turning to a consideration of the capabilities of the young learner, observation of children at the ages of five and six indicates that their reactions and interests are spontaneous and immediate. They tend to centre on that which they are doing at a particular moment, and activity rather than passivity is their preferred mode of behaviour. Their skill in considering the whole in terms of its parts and the parts in terms of the whole – an essential mental strategy in word analysis and identification – is at a very early stage of development, and they are not very much concerned with abstractions: they see things in terms of what they know. For example, they see God as a long-haired, bewhiskered, kindly old man, and ghosts as humans in sheets.

These behavioural and cognitive constraints have important implications for teaching, and any methodology which does not seek to allow for them in the teaching techniques, rather than to ignore them, may soon find itself in difficulties.

Unfortunately, much of our present methodology in the teaching of reading does in fact fail to make things easy for the learner. Reading books take the child to experiences which are remote from his immediate preoccupations in the classroom and which are frequently remote from his concept of the world – dreary, uninteresting accounts of family life in suburbia, lacking in imagination and devoid of any literary quality. Furthermore, where these texts lack a strong and tightly-written theme, so necessary if the reader is to be able to make informed guesses and predict unknown words, the child's weakest skills are engaged: namely, his analytical skills and his power of memory for abstractions, whilst his stronger skills such as his ability to follow a line of thought and his ability to understand language are forced to remain dormant.

To elaborate upon this argument, the phonic analysis of words requires two things: analytical skill, which does not come easily to five- and six-year-old children (Roberts 1975), and the development of the skill of clustering based on basic spelling patterns (Gibson *et al.* 1970), which is a specific form of analysis which obviously must be used discriminatingly, and which only emerges gradually because it is a factor of increasing familiarity with the formation of words. (These two things are not in any way helped in those teaching situations where there is an emphasis on the individual letter sounds of words. In fact, in those situations much of the teaching is useless, and it is only the child's ability to sort things out for himself that carries him slowly forward. Neither are they helped by simply telling the child to cluster the letters. He must be shown examples from which he can draw his own comparisons.)

Returning to the main argument that teaching techniques frequently require the child to rely upon skills of phonic analysis, which are the weakest of his language skills because they are as yet undeveloped, the result is that when these fail him, he is thrown back upon his memory for discrete words. Now it is obvious that skilled readers remember hundreds of discrete words, but this is not the case with children who are beginning to learn to read. Certainly they will remember some words, but it is reasonable to suppose that those that they remember will be those that have attracted their attention because they have been encountered in a memorable context and themselves refer to something tangible, vivid and vital to the children. It would not be reasonable to suppose that those words which occur most frequently in the prose of early reading books, words such as *like, come, is, here, there, play*, etc., fall into the category of vivid, vital words. One does not hear children repeating them spontaneously as is the case with swear words, catch phrases, jingles and rhymes. Hence, the young reader is virtually forced to rely upon his memory for the least memorable of words, and thus he reads in a hesitant and halting manner and, when both his phonic skill and his memory let him down, he cannot turn to his knowledge of language in order to extract meaning from the text that he is reading because the semantic constraints within that text are not tight enough to enable him to solve the problem of the un-

c

recognized word from the meaning of the text. Thus the texts of the majority of early reading books used in the United Kingdom do not help the beginner, and the child who is beginning to learn to read does not have the skills necessary to handle those texts. Therefore, it must follow that a major shift in the methodology for teaching children to read is necessary.

The rationale for a new methodological approach can be simply stated. Texts should be provided which help the young learner by utilizing his stronger rather than his weaker skills in the first place. These stronger skills are concerned with the interpretation of language, which emerge from his familiarity with the use of language as a means of communication. The child entering school has at least a working facility in the English language and has the propensity to acquire a tremendous range of language patterns if they are fostered in a supportive context, *viz*. his ability to handle and enjoy the different patterns within nursery rhymes, well-written folk stories and jingles of all kinds.

Naturally, as the learner progresses so the objectives of the texts should change. Gradually the child's weaker skills – those concerned with the abstract nature of word construction and analysis, the syllabic, morphenic and pronounceable boundaries within words – should be developed through the provision of exemplars of various letter formations in ways which allow comparisons to be drawn between words. Emphasis should be given to discovering comparisons between words which have common elements and to tracing the effects of lexical context upon specific letters and letter combinations, such as the irregular letters (*a, e, i, o, u, c, g* and *s*) and digraphs (especially the vowel digraphs).

Where possible during the early stages, an imposed analytical attack upon words should be avoided and stress should be placed upon building up words from known parts. Again, this can best be done through comparisons of words containing some common element. Thus, the young child would not be expected to carry out those 'actions' (concerned with analysis) which he finds more difficult than others, such as synthesis (Roberts 1975) from known elements by means of comparisons drawn for himself.

An 'emergent' reading programme
In a short paper of this nature, the framework for a new integrated

methodology incorporating all aspects of language can only be outlined briefly. (A fuller exposition is given in Cashdan, A. (ed.) *Teaching a Language for Life* Blackwell (1978).) It is assumed that this framework will be preceded by the type of activities suggested in Moira McKenzie's paper in this volume, in which she writes of an 'emergent reading programme' – a term both evocative and precise which could usefully replace the looser term 'pre-reading activities', and which would include the first two steps in the following proposals.

The first step in a methodology which integrates the various aspects of language and reading would be to use the child's language as it emerges from his immediate activities and actions within the classroom. The teacher's Sentence Maker in *Breakthrough to Literacy* (Schools Council 1970) is an ideal piece of apparatus, because it can be used as a group activity. This will allow an original statement by one child to be taken up as the basis for group discussion, out of which will emerge several variations on the original statement, and all of which will be transposed by the teacher into written texts through the use of *Breakthrough* cards and the large trough in which the cards can be placed.

The element of group interaction is very important, because it is through this that alterations and adjustments can be made to the various oral statements offered by members of the group. In this way, the children will not only witness the construction of prose but they will be introduced to the possibilities of manipulating language to meet various exigencies. Thus, their increased awareness of the nature of print will not be left to chance as has been the case with the older methodology.

The second step will be the introduction of the beginner to books, but not books where in order to 'read' he has to rely upon phonic skills and upon his memory for abstractions. The books should contain stories already known to the child, so that the young reader can follow the meaning and use it for purposes of anticipation. If the texts contain nursery rhymes and folk stories known by the child, then by 'reading' these *with the teacher* the child will be gaining further evidence that print is another way of conveying ideas that are already in his mind. Hence reading will be seen purely as an extension of those communication skills already possessed by the learner, rather than a totally new skill to be acquired from scratch. The psychological implications of this would be immense. It would create confidence in the learner, and it would take much of the mystique out of reading.

Again, most of the reading at this stage could be done as a group activity, with all the group seeking to match the words to the rhymes and stories that they are simultaneously recalling. With this procedure the child tackles his first reading book with the help of others, rather than alone and in isolation. Hence he sees his problems as common ones instead of regarding them as unique to himself.

At the third step the activity will revert back to the group construction of prose, only this time the phrases and words which have been learned from the nursery rhymes, folk stories and jingles will be added to the *Breakthrough* word bank, and stories connected with them can now be constructed by the group. Instead of stories based upon the actions of the children, as was the case at step one, the stories at this step will be based upon stories that they have recalled and 'read' at step two. This will correspond with the widening interests of children as they move from centring solely upon their own activities to the happenings in the world around them. It is a further step in their training in the composition and interpretation of texts.

Step four would introduce the child to the more exacting study of sentences, phrases, and words within those phrases and sentences that have already been used in the first three steps. In addition these should be compared and contrasted with sentences, phrases and words taken from the literature that is to follow at steps five and six. Thus we have words from a familiar context being studied alongside words from an unfamiliar context. This will help the reader to widen his field of language and word study. (It is crucially important that language study is regarded as part of learning to read; most of the methodologies of the past have been concerned only with the study of words, and even then almost entirely from the point of view of the letter patterns rather than meaning.)

Step five would find the child ready to read connected prose in which the story content is not known, but where many of the sentences, phrases and words are familiar. In order to ensure that the child will be meeting familiar words, etc., it will be necessary for the teacher to compose the stories himself – a time-consuming task, but not an impossible one even in the first instance, and becoming progressively easier as a collection of these stories is built up over the years.

Step six would see the introduction of published texts – graded readers minus the inane first books, specialized schemes such as *Skylarks*, *Mount Gravatt Readers* and children's literature as found in the Puffin books. Much of the reading will be in the form of an individual activity by the child, but the teacher should not forget the advantages of group study. The Bullock Report points to the value of group discussions about a particular book or passage and to the opportunities to develop a deeper understanding of features of the language.

Within these six steps the unknown elements are closely controlled for the learner. At first the story content is known and the smaller units of language are fitted into the overall story pattern, whereas at the later steps, when the child has had time to acquire a familiarity with segments of language such as short sentences, phrases and words, he then has to turn his attention to acquiring the meaning of the text. Thus he is taken from the known to the unknown at each part of the scheme, and the unknown elements are severely restricted. The whole approach is language based rather than word based, activity based rather than sight based, and is group supportive rather than based on the individually isolated learner. The steps are sequential but not exclusive; for example, language enrichment and word study, which form the basis of step four, are occurring at every step in varying degrees and forms. Hence within the framework it is possible to build a language programme in which all the elements are integrated and reading no longer stands apart as an isolated skill.

Quick reference outline

Steps	Activity
1	Oral composition and 'reading'. (*Breakthrough* activities based on child's actions.)
2	Recall of stories, matching and 'reading'. (Nursery rhymes, folk stories and jingles.)

3   Oral composition and reading.
        (*Breakthrough* activities based on stories.)

4   Awareness of written language patterns, including
        phrase and word study.
        (Language from preceding and subsequent steps.)

5   Reading fairly constrained material.
        (Reading stories written by the teacher.)

6   Reading unconstrained material.
        (Reading published works of literature.)

References

BEVINGTON, J. and CRYSTAL, D. (1975) *Skylarks* Nelson
CASHDAN, A. (Ed.) (1978) *Teaching a Language for Life* Blackwell
GIBSON, E. J. *et al* (1970) 'Utilization of spelling patterns by deaf and
    hearing subjects' in H. Levin and J. P. Williams (eds) *Basic Studies on
    Reading* New York: Basic Books
HUEY, E. B. (1908) *The Psychology and Pedagogy of Reading* New York:
    Macmillan (reprinted in 1968, 1972 and 1973 by M.I.T. Press)
ROBERTS, T. (1975) Skills of analysis and synthesis in the early stages of
    reading *British Journal of Educational Psychology* 45, 3–9
SCHOOLS COUNCIL (1970) *Breakthrough to Literacy* Longman

5 Organizing resources for learning to read in the primary school

Bridie Raban

The need for a 'master-plan'

It is one thing to have an array of materials and techniques . . . ;
it is quite another to be able to put these together coherently to
provide an appropriate reading curriculum for each individual
child as well as for the class as a whole. This calls for clear
thinking about sequence and structure. (Bullock Report, 7.30)

It has been shown from the evidence of the results of remedial
work that children respond well to carefully-structured and
sequenced programmes of work; their reading ability as well as
their attitude towards reading improves. It would appear, therefore, that most children could benefit from such an approach and
teachers would also find it more helpful to work to a 'master-plan'
(Southgate 1970) which would guide their decisions in this curriculum area.

Any kind of planned programme of work must be thought out
in such a way that it ensures that specified goals are achieved, and
the elements in the programme will reflect this. In order to set up
such a programme, then, it is necessary to decide what it is you are
trying to teach the children to do. This question is not as easy to
answer as it superficially appears. Consider the definitions of the
reading process which appear in the Bullock Report (6.5):

1 a response to graphic signals in terms of the words they
   represent
2 a response to text in terms of the meanings the author intended to set down
3 a response to the author's meanings in terms of all the relevant
   previous experience and present judgments of the reader.

If we adopt definition 3 as our goal, which seems to absorb and supercede definitions 1 and 2, we are unlikely to achieve it if we concentrate all our teaching towards encouraging the children to respond to graphic signals in terms of the words they represent. Of course they need to do this successfully, but they need to do more than this if they are to become readers in the fuller sense of definition 3. Whilst, as has been suggested, teaching techniques may reflect the priority of any one of these three definitions at different times during the programme, it remains important that the overall plan reflects the more fundamental attitude to reading in the sense of definition 3. This may seem too obvious for explicit statement but the question 'What is reading?' is still one for professional debate.

Consider the variety of professional associations which discuss the reading curriculum: for instance, the School Library Association, the National Association of Teachers of English, the United Kingdom Reading Association. Consider also the alignment of the Bullock Report definitions, referred to earlier, as they relate to these associations. Teachers need access to the ideas from all such professional associations; they need to synthesize as many different approaches as possible. It is in this way that teachers develop and extend their own theories of the reading process. They must try and remain open and responsive to ideas from as many sources as possible and develop fresh procedures in the classrooms. In one sense, everything that is said about children learning to read has something of value to offer the teacher; in another sense it is the individual teachers themselves who know best what will work for them and their children. From these two bases classroom procedures will be improved.

From what has been said above, it is clear that any guidelines for the organization of resources for children learning to read in the primary school that are presented in this paper must be seen as the view of an individual teacher; although many of the ideas for its development have come from discussion with colleagues and work with children as well as from studying many of the points of view which surround the teaching of reading. These ideas are presented as a starting point for anyone faced with the problem of organizing resources, and many teachers who have adopted this approach have developed and changed it to suit their own needs and those of their children. This, then, is the purpose of teachers sharing ideas and what follows is by way of a systematic description of one approach to the problems of organization.

No one is clear about how children learn to read; all that is known for certain is that the ability will develop more rapidly the more opportunities a child has for successful reading. The implications of this are that children need access to books they know they can read as well as others which are well within their competence and others still which could be assumed to be too difficult.

The suitability of reading material

If a teacher is to plan individual instruction to meet specific needs, her first task is to assess the attainment level of every child and provide each with reading material of the right level of readability. (Bullock Report 17.19)

This paragraph in the Bullock Report continues by describing the *independent, instructional* and *frustration* levels of reading materials and how these can be assessed with respect to individual children's reading performance. This concept, when related to books graded for difficulty (Moon 1973), can ensure that classroom collections of books can be organized to the advantage of both children and teacher.

Individualised Reading (Moon 1973) is a list of selected books for primary-school children, graded according to difficulty. These lists are annually revised and updated and include both fiction and non-fiction. Criteria regarding the suitability of such books for novice readers have been discussed fully elsewhere (Moon and Raban 1975). Essentially, what teachers need to consider for each book in turn is:

1 Is the book 'easy' to read in the sense that it helps the child to develop useful strategies?
2 Is the book unduly biased, so as to emphasize certain attitudes at the expense of others?
3 Most important of all, is the book worth the effort?

When choosing books for the class collection it must be remembered that there is more to reading than meets the eye, and selec-

Table 1 **Individualised Reading: description of the stage progression** (from Moon 1973)

Stage	Description (from Moon and Raban 1975)
0	Pure picture books (no text) which follow a clear, unambiguous sequence, e.g. *Changes, Changes* (Hutchins (1971) Bodley Head).
1	'Caption books' where *phrase* matches illustration with minimum ambiguity. Text is usually under illustration, e.g. *First Words* (Southgate (1968) Macmillan).
2	'Caption books' where *sentence* matches illustration. Usually one-word changes in each page and that word should be obvious from the focal point of the illustration, e.g. *This is My Colour, This is My Shape* (Thackray (1973) George Philip Alexander).
3	'Caption books' which have more varied text. The child will now have to pay more attention to the text although the illustrations are essential, e.g. *Super Butch Books* (Le Jeune (1977) Cassell).
4, 5, 6	Less and less dependence on illustrations and consequently text is fairly limited, vocabulary range is narrow within a particular book. New words should be obvious from the illustration. Ideally a text form which is compatible with oral language development is used, e.g. *Little Books* (Burningham (1974) Cape).
7, 8, 9	'Developmental reading'. Stories becoming longer, print smaller, style conforming to standard written form, wider vocabulary content. Most books are still short enough to be read at a sitting. Ideally these books are phrased in print format according to 'units of meaning', e.g. *Monster Books* (Blance and Cook (1973) Longman).
10	'Consolidation books'. Short, well-illustrated books with wide vocabulary. This is the point at which most reading schemes end, e.g. *Help Story Books* (Webster (1974) Nelson).
11, 12, 13	'Bridging books'. Developmental bridging from short, amply-illustrated books to longer books (fiction in chapters) which do not rely on illustration cues. When children can read fluently books from stage 13, they should be able to succeed with the wealth of fiction available to them (e.g. the Puffin range). A good guide to the three 'bridging' stages are Hamish Hamilton's *Gazelle*, *Antelope* and *Reindeer* series.

tions must be made with worked-out criteria in mind (McKenzie and Warlow 1977).

Both from experience and research evidence (Wells and Raban forthcoming) it appears to be the case that approximately one-third of novice readers need explicit help with the subskills of reading and they need their attention drawn to specific features of print if they are to internalize a model of the way print works. Semantic and syntactic cues all contribute towards the identification of the graphic display, which relates directly to the meaning of the prose. But inevitably no such accuracy can be achieved if the reader has no detailed knowledge of the elements in the graphic display. Although the majority of children are able to achieve this through their experience of print alone, other children need activities designed to ensure that they do read with sufficient accuracy. It is because of this that further lists of selected non-book resources (Raban 1974) have been developed to complement the book reading programme outlined above.

Adapting the plan to individual needs
The non-book resources have been listed across four main levels, A–D, and against areas of skill, 1–4. As shown in Table 2, the book-reading programme is related to this developmental sequence by the stage numbers marked in the left-hand column.

Although the subskills marked in each box of Table 2 appear relatively straightforward, there has been an amount of discussion and even controversy as to what do constitute the subskills of reading. For instance, with respect to auditory discrimination the Bullock Report states:

> Contrary to popular belief, the majority of children are perfectly capable, well before they start school, of making the perceptual discriminations necessary for learning letter shapes. They learn to make extremely complex auditory discriminations in language . . .
> We do not believe that a formal programme of training in auditory discrimination as such will significantly advance reading readiness. (6.15; 7.10)

Margaret Clark's research (1976) on young fluent readers – children who were reading before they started school – suggests

Table 2 Reading skill acquisition programme for primary schools (from Moon and Raban (1975))

Level	Description	Area 1	Area 2	Area 3	Area 4
A I. R. Stages, 0, 1, 2, 3	Preliteracy and beginning reading.	1 Language development and concept formation. 2 Speech-to-print, transition.	Auditory discrimination.	Visual discrimination.	Development of motor skills.
B I. R. Stages, 4, 5, 6	Early reading.	Use of context. Whole-word recognition and vocabulary-extension work.	Early 'phonic' work: 1 initial letters 2 final letters.	1 c→vc. 2 cv→c. 3 three-letter words.	Letter formation. Handwriting.
C I. R. Stages, 7, 8, 9	Word analysis and synthesis.	Further development of prediction skills.	'Phonic' development work: 1 mid vowels a e i o u 2 final consonant clusters 3 initial consonant clusters 4 long vowel.		Spelling.
D I. R. Stages, 10, 11, 12, 13	Reading (for pleasure and information).	Development of study skills and critical reading.			

Note:
I. R. refers to Individualized Reading (Moon 1973)
c=consonant
v=vowel

that many perceptual readiness-for-reading tests were failed by the children in her study. These qualifications are equally true of visual perception and it seems obvious that perceptual skills *per se* are not necessarily what the child needs to develop, but rather the conceptual skills pertinent to reading print and the ways in which the features of print correspond to meaning. This does not imply that the activities traditionally referred to as 'pre-reading' are irrelevant, rather that shape-matching and sound-identification tasks are not directly related to later achievement in reading, but more appropriately considered as aspects of the curriculum which help the child learn to learn and settle into the new environment of the classroom, both very important prerequisites for learning to read. Similarly, at Level B, the novice-reader needs to be able to use his knowledge of the sound/symbol system, but how he acquires this knowledge is not at all clear:

> The question, then, is not whether or not to teach phonics; of this there can be no doubt. The question is when and how to do it. (Bullock Report 6.23)

Telling a child the sounds of the letters does not appear to be appropriate; it seems more helpful to use activities which *inevitably* develop the child's awareness of such relationships, and it is important to check that such activities do indeed help the child to gain insight into the complex interrelationship of phonemes and graphemes.

Essentially, the grapho–phonemic cueing system must remain secondary to the semantic and syntactic cueing systems. The child's ability to use language at all will always help to carry the burden of the one-to-many and many-to-one correspondences in the sound/symbol system. With the child's growing ability to smoothly predict and check whilst reading (Clay 1972a), his ability to operate both cueing systems simultaneously will develop and increase his skill. Whilst it is true to say that the child learns to read, it is also important to stress the reciprocal function of the teacher as she controls the reading experiences and activities for each child.

Finally, a cautionary note needs emphasis. Any systematic organization of resources must be for the teacher's benefit primarily. For, as Marie Clay (1972b) has pointed out:

Observation of children suggests that they do not learn about language on any one level of organization *before* they manipulate units at higher levels. (Many teaching schemes imply that this is so.) . . . As the child learns to (read and) write there is a rich intermingling of language learning *across* levels which probably accounts in some way for the fast progress which the best children can make. A simplification achieved by dealing firstly with letters, then with words and finally with word groups may be easy for teachers to understand but children learn on all levels at once. (p. 19)

Any contrivance on the part of the teacher which makes all children experience all the steps of the programme will not be responding to their needs. The master-plan is best seen as a back-cloth against which individual decisions can be made concerning each child:

The major difference between teachers lies not in their allegiance to a method but in the quality of their relationships with children, their degree of expert knowledge and their sensitivity in matching what they do to each child's current learning needs. (Bullock Report 7.20)

References

DES (1975) *A Language for Life* (The Bullock Report) HMSO
CLARK, M. M. (1976) *Young Fluent Readers* Heinemann
CLAY, M. M. (1972a) *Reading: the Patterning of Complex Behaviour* Heinemann
CLAY, M. M. (1972b) *What Did I Write?* Heinemann
McKENZIE, M. and WARLOW, A. (1977) *Reading Matters* Hodder and Stoughton in association with ILEA
MOON, C. (1973) *Individualised Reading* Centre for the Teaching of Reading, University of Reading
MOON, C. and RABAN, B. (1975) *A Question of Reading* Ward Lock Educational
RABAN, B. (1974) *Reading Skill Acquisition* Centre for the Teaching of Reading, University of Reading
SOUTHGATE, V. (1970) *Beginning Reading* Hodder and Stoughton
WELLS, G. and RABAN, B. (forthcoming) *Children Learning to Read* Final Report SSRC Research Project HR 3797/1

6 Equal opportunity in reading

Lawrence W. Carrillo

Introduction

One of the things you will find on most employment application forms in the United States is a statement to the effect that this employer is an 'equal opportunity employer'. This means that you will have an equal opportunity for the job, considering only your abilities for that job, but *not* considering your race, creed, colour or sex. I am for equal opportunity in all things, including the learning of reading skills. But, it seems to me, many children have not been afforded this democratic principle. They have been presented with the involved task of formal reading before they were ready, thus destroying not only *that* opportunity, but many in the future.

Please consider this quotation:

> . . . If it be not, 'tis not to come; if it be not to come, it will be now; if it be not now, yet it will come; the readiness is all. (*Hamlet*, Act V, Scene 2)

Any educator who has examined the records of poor readers in intermediate or upper grades will realize that these problems began early. Most records of poor readers show a lack of readiness in kindergarten and first grade. Reading skills were then attempted on an infirm foundation, and were not successfully achieved. Readiness must come first: 'If it be not, 'tis not to come'. If readiness is not present when formal reading instruction is started, good reading skills cannot result.

To give the other side, as Shakespeare did, there are a number of children who have acquired enough of the aspects of reading readiness by kindergarten age to begin reading successfully at that point: '. . . if it be not to come, it will be now'. Many are ready *now*.

The numbers of children who are ready to begin formal reading instruction at the age of five are, as a rough estimate, about one in five. But those children are so obvious, and do so well, that we are tempted to begin many others who have not yet achieved sufficient readiness. This is simply another example of individual differences. What has happened to each of them and how they have absorbed it compounds the original differences between and among children. In the United States, for some reason, we seem to feel that earlier and more means better. It does not. Since the normal human reaction to failure is either to fight or to back off, that is what happens to children who are given too much too soon. They either become aggressive to school, schoolmates, teachers and books, or they refuse to try, and take all the avoidance reactions possible.

Therefore, those who are not ready should receive great variety of readiness instruction rather than formal reading. Again, as Shakespeare pointed out: '. . . if it be not now, yet it will come'. However, it does not ordinarily come just through time only, but through gradually increasing maturity which is a result of careful instruction. Waiting is not enough, neither is expecting a child, who cannot yet count to five, to learn all of the letters of the alphabet, since there are fifty-two of them, counting capitals.

Ordinarily, learning comes by small steps, and there is a great deal of forgetting in the process. Too much formal reading instruction too soon is an invitation to trouble, both for the child and for the school; and an important aspect of the concept of readiness is the part that says you must be ready to take the next step, no matter where you are in the process. So even the teacher above first-grade level, or infant school, must be concerned with readiness. If a child at any grade level (or even an adult) finds that the thing that you are asking him to do is far beyond him, he will ordinarily either think you are stupid for asking so much, or he simply avoids the task. So '. . . the readiness is all' – at all levels.

After that introduction, it may be time for a definition of reading readiness. *Readiness is the stage of developmental maturity at which a child can learn to read (or take the next step in reading) easily, effectively, and without much personal disturbance.*

There is one problem with that definition: it is an after-the-fact definition. If the child was not ready, he fails; if he was ready, he succeeds easily and well. But the very thing we wish to avoid is the failure, so the definition is not much help.

Factors

What is of more help is a knowledge of the factors which tend to be important in readiness, and there are, of course, tests and checklists to help teachers evaluate the child's status in regard to these factors. No listing of these factors, however, can show relative importance, since that factor which may be of high importance to one may be relatively minor for another. Still, some are rather basic and a few are listed below (from Carrillo 1971).

I *Intellectual factors*
(a) Sufficient mental capacity, as shown by ability to:
  1 use oral language well; speak in sentences, utilize a variety of words
  2 answer verbal questions and follow simple verbal directions
  3 remember happenings of previous days or weeks and change present behaviour through the remembering
  4 classify objects according to general categories
  5 think independently to solve problems
  6 shift from one sensory modality to another – particularly auditory–visual shift.
(b) Adequate auditory and visual discrimination, as shown by ability to:
  1 recognize likenesses and differences in sound at the beginning and ending of words
  2 recognize likenesses and differences in shape, size, position and colour; observe relatively small details.

II *Physical factors*
(a) Normal vision, including:
  1 good visual acuity, adequate fusion, good eye-muscle control
  2 improving eye–hand coordination
  3 adequate colour discrimination (note the boys on this particularly).

(b) Normal hearing.
(c) Adequate speech-sound production (articulation of language sounds and the avoidance of slurring or baby talk).
(d) Normal general health and vitality:
1 no lingering illnesses
2 normal energy level
3 good general motor control
4 consistent sleep habits.
(e) Kinesthetic awareness of his own body.

III *Emotional factors*
(a) Self-control and self-reliance, as shown by:
1 growing independence, balanced by need for adult approval
2 some aggressiveness, competitiveness, boastfulness.
(b) Initiative and ambition.
(c) Some respect for the rights of others, shown by:
1 listening attentively to others
2 forming friendships
3 working in a group.
(d) Positive attitude towards learning to read.
(e) Eagerness to hear stories and tell stories.
(f) Participation in cooperative ventures.
(g) Freedom from severe speech disabilities.

IV *Environmental factors*
(a) Liberal background of facts and concepts.
(b) Home that values school and reading.
(c) English language background enough so that basic vocabulary has real meaning.
(d) Experience with books and some practice in handling books.
(e) Home experiences in responsibility.
(f) Neighbourhood where he has friends of about the same age.

V *Educational factors*
(a) Adjustment to the school situation, as shown by:
1 little crying due to separation or fears
2 ability to attend ordinarily to physical needs

3 mostly sensible behaviour on playground and in class-room.

(b) Ability to handle basic school tasks:
1 handle a crayon or brush at easel and desk
2 handle books without tearing
3 listen to directions and follow them
4 listen to stories and enjoy them.

(c) Good attitude towards school and teachers, as shown by:
1 not hiding under tables, or otherwise showing fear
2 absence of physical aggression towards teacher
3 appreciation of what teachers can do.

Such a listing may seem too long, but it could be made even longer. Every teacher of young children must be conscious of these factors and work towards the development of them if each child is to have an equal opportunity to succeed in reading.

Materials

One of the things important in the development of readiness is the materials which are used. There are paper-covered workbooks designed to precede basal readers; there are informal tasks directed by the teacher; there are teacher-made materials; there are games, spirit-duplicator masters of exercises, boxes of materials for flannel-board and chalk-board, and plastic manipulative devices and puppets of all kinds. What to use? All I can offer are a few cautions and suggestions to the teacher.

1 The first consideration in the choice of readiness materials or activities is whether or not they help develop specific, neces-sary readiness skills. The objectives of the teacher, the particular reading programme used in the school and the specific needs of the children control the choice of materials and the approaches.

When all of the children have mastered a particular skill, then it needs only maintenance, not further emphasis. The largest needs of the group should determine the emphasis, not the preferences of the teacher.

2 Exercises should be chosen so that they contribute and are not boring 'busy work'. Activities that merely keep children

busy (skills already mastered), should be used mainly as success experiences when other learning tasks have been difficult or when maintenance of a skill is desired.

3 Activities should first develop *thinking* skills that are directly associated with reading. Any exercise that is merely activity without associated meaning contributes very little.

4 Pre-reading diagnosis, on readiness tests or checklists or through observation, yields planning for individuals. Observing the use of such things as readiness books yields clues as to which children will need to move at slower and at faster rates. Grouping and individualization begin early, but should be done with information.

Be sure to choose materials which have accompanying diagnostic approaches and instructions for interpreting them.

5 Highly coloured materials are not as necessary as we tend to believe. Children want realism. Look at your printed readiness activities, not bright colour for realism.

6 It is not necessary to have all young children together all the time. Whenever possible, form readiness groupings (two, three or four per classroom) so that each group can do more essential activities at a pace they can stand. Naturally, there will be many individual problems, so plan time for them. There is no great hurry . . .

7 Please remember that the five or six year old has a very short attention span. *Any* activity or exercise should be short; those for more immature children should probably take no longer than ten minutes.

8 Reinforcement of learning – immediate commendation for a job well done – should occur immediately after a task is finished. Immediate feedback is a real key for the child – he knows whether or not to do that same thing again.

9 It is a good policy to use more readiness activities and materials after formal reading instruction has started. It is even better to be *more* than ready.

In the final analysis, we are working with ways of thinking. Such thinking skills must be maintained and reinforced to be perfected. This practice does *not* represent a loss of curricular time.

10 Try to find as many manipulative materials as you can, so the

children may move around often. Almost any pencil-and-paper exercise can be converted to a manipulative task.

11 Try to avoid the purple haze resulting from too much spirit-duplicator material. This is not what I meant earlier by avoiding highly coloured materials – if you are stuck with the necessity of using duplicated materials often, get some of the black, the red or the green duplicator masters.

12 Look to your objectives. Do not merely choose materials which add to language skills – you are developing a *whole child*.

Strengthen:
visual discrimination
basic visual ability
motor and eye–hand coordination
ability to differentiate colours
left-to-right progression in eye movement and work patterns
desire to read
auditory perception
listening habits
kinesthetic awareness of one's own body and its relationship to surroundings
breadth and depth of experiential background
comprehension of relationships (comparison, contrast, classification)
positive adjustment to school situations.

These are very general suggestions, and they must be, because children (and teachers) differ.

Conclusion
Very little of this is at all new. Perhaps the newness is that it is a return to former thinking and values in regard to the teaching of children. Here is a quotation from Schonell (1945):

Young immature minds need opportunity and time to 'sort things out', to understand what they are doing, and to see the purpose in the operations with which they are confronted. My strongest plea in the teaching of reading is, don't hurry the children, don't expect too much in the early stages – do all you can to provide a language background. This slower, wider approach will repay doubly later on.

And here is a truly remarkable passage from Rousseau's *Émile*:

We usually obtain very surely and very quickly what we are in no haste to obtain. I am almost certain that Émile will know how to read and write perfectly before the age of ten, precisely because I care but very little whether he learns these things before the age of fifteen. I would much rather he would never know how to read than to buy this knowledge at the price of all that can make it useful. Of what use would reading be to him after he had been disgusted with it forever?

There you have the point. The readiness is all when it comes to equal opportunity to learn and equal opportunity for later enjoyment and use.

Much is built on the readiness foundation, therefore that foundation must be solid, otherwise the whole thing collapses.

References

CARRILLO, L. W. (1971) *Informal Reading Readiness Experiences* New York: Noble and Noble

CARRILLO, L. W. (1976) *Teaching Reading: A Handbook* New York: St Martin's Press

ROUSSEAU, J.-J. (1893) *Émile* translated by W. H. Payne. New York: Appleton-Century-Crofts

SCHONELL, F. J. (1945) *The Psychology and Teaching of Reading* Oliver and Boyd

7 Selecting literature for the language development of young children

Betty Coody

That positive steps be taken to develop the language ability of children in preschool, nursery and infant years was one of the principal recommendations made by the Bullock Committee. For those persons committed to the belief that successful reading is based on oral language facility, it may well be the most significant recommendation in the Report.

We know that a rich programme of literature for young children, directly aimed at language fluency, is one of the most effective ways to prepare them for a smooth beginning in reading and, subsequently, for successful independent reading later on. Children begin to view reading as an important and integral part of their lives when respected adults are skilful at selecting and sharing appropriate literature with them by means of reading aloud, storytelling, dramatization, puppetry, discussions, field trips and other book-related activities.

In choosing books to use with young children, both parents and teachers should become familiar with the various types of literature that appeal most to the preschoolers – books that are so well written and beautifully illustrated that they seem inherently to meet the basic needs of early childhood. Moreover, with money for books so difficult to come by, it is wise to develop a plan of priority buying until a varied and quality collection has been acquired. If a few books are purchased each year from the different classifications, it is possible for even the smallest library to be a well-balanced one. Needless to say, a few really excellent books are worth more to the language development of a young child than any number of trite and inane publications. (Examples of some of the favourite editions from each of the following categories are listed in the bibliography.)

Mother Goose

The practice of saying and singing nursery rhymes to children is an ancient one; it is, at the same time, as modern as tomorrow. Friendly characters acting out their exciting adventures, humorous and nonsensical situations, repetitive and rhythmic language hold the same appeal for today's children as for those of past generations. Mother Goose rhymes have been aptly called the 'perfect literature of childhood'. When presented to children on a regular basis, they not only help to develop in children a feeling for the poetic and musical quality of language, but a sense of story as well. Both home and classroom book collections should contain as many editions of Mother Goose as the budget will allow.

Alphabet books

The main purpose of an ABC book is to teach a young child the alphabet, but it also presents familiar objects and animals for consideration and discussion. A few key words are included as labels for the pictures. Parents and teachers often use such books for beginning phonics instruction as they teach the sound each letter represents.

Many beautiful ABC books are available on the market today, some illustrated with photography and others by means of realistic paintings or semi-abstract art. In any case, an ABC book should be attractively simple with only one or two familiar objects on each uncluttered page, with the letter itself standing out in bold relief.

Counting books

Counting books are used with young children mainly to acquaint them with the language and some of the basic symbolism of mathematics. When selecting counting books, the same high standards should apply as with ABC books. Each numeral should stand alone on its own page, accompanied only by those forms and shapes needed to illustrate the concept represented by the numeral. Objects to be counted should be clearly delineated and set apart to avoid confusion, and none of the pages should be crowded or cluttered with too many pictures.

Concept books

As the vocabulary of a young child increases, so does the interest in abstract concepts or generalized ideas. Phenomena such as size, shape, speed, weight, time, distance, mass and colour are presented to children in graphic, artistic form. Since only a few of the concept books are written with a story line, teachers usually find it best to read them aloud to small groups or to individual children, and to explain and clarify as they go. Of course, concept books are excellent material for parents to use at home while reading to one child. Questions may be answered and the parent is in a good position to point out and explain the more obscure meanings.

Concept books should be chosen with extreme care if they are to coincide with the maturity level of a child. A concept book should never be forced upon the child. If it does not appeal, it should be put away until a later date when the child is more likely to accept the thoughts presented.

Machines personified

A modern author who depicts machines personified is simply updating a primitive belief that most inanimate objects possess a spirit or personality. Such stories are usually inspirational in nature, since the plot is built around some staggering, over-whelming task to be accomplished by the machine. After much effort and suspense, the task is performed successfully and the machine is highly respected for its achievement.

In selecting books about machines personified, the teacher or parent should first look for a story of high adventure in which the machine stays true to its own character even though personified – a steam shovel, for example, must continue to look like a steam shovel and it should continue to perform the tasks of a steam shovel.

Animal stories

Talking-beast tales are extremely popular with young children – tales in which both wise and foolish animals act very much like human beings. Such stories are often called 'ourselves in fur'. We see animals work, play, laugh, cry, make foolish mistakes and perform acts of kindness and wisdom. Such stories are ideal for reading aloud and storytelling since they can be approached from the storyteller's own viewpoint and changed accordingly. Very little memorization is necessary.

Most talking-beast tales contain a great deal of dialogue which children like to hear, to imitate and to read for themselves later on. As was previously mentioned in regard to machines personified, animals must remain true to their own kind, even though they talk, if young children are going to accept them as friends and learn from them.

Humour and nonsense

Every classroom should contain an ample supply of books that are guaranteed to give children a hearty laugh. Laughter is therapeutic and a wonderful release from tedious mental tasks. It is no surprise that children request their favourite books of humour and nonsense to be read aloud again and again.

People and animals in absurd, incongruous situations strike children as funny, and they especially enjoy watching story characters use logic and cunning to work themselves out of one ludicrous dilemma after another. Interestingly, these are the same stories adults seem to prefer reading aloud to children. Perhaps we all see ourselves in similar inevitable crises brought about by human frailty, but at the same time resolved by human ingenuity.

To read aloud excellent stories of humour and nonsense on a regular basis is a way to make certain that children have a good time with literature.

Picture books

Picture books are those in which the illustrations play such an important part that the text would be incomplete without them. Though some picture books are wordless, most contain a few sentences on each page, perfectly synchronized with the pictures so that a pre-reading child is able to follow along as the story is being read aloud.

Young children who learn to care about picture books turn to them for information and enjoyment over and over again during the first years in school, and they are the same people who continue to appreciate fine book illustrations even into adulthood.

Studying pictures is an extension of reading that adds immeasurably to comprehension at all levels.

Beautiful picture books that employ many techniques, styles and media provide the young child with an introduction to the world of art. For this reason, only the best should be selected for school use. After all, a child's taste in art and literature is being permanently influenced.

Easy-to-read books

Books are classified as 'easy-to-read' or 'beginner' books if they employ a controlled vocabulary of frequently-used words. Only a few words are used and they are repeated throughout the text. The words are basically the same as those found in pre-primers and primers.

Since easy-to-read trade books are rather new to the publishing scene, many teachers remember when there were practically no materials other than textbooks that they could offer to their beginning pupils for independent reading. But more and more books are being written for fledgeling readers and they are proving to be quite popular with children and teachers as well. The teachers recognize that repetition of basic sight words, presented in the context of an entertaining story, prompts independent reading practice needed by beginning readers.

Controlled vocabulary books have been called artless by some critics but, understandably, young children are grateful for anything they can read themselves. For this reason alone, easy-to-read books are justified. If a conscientious teacher continues to read aloud from excellent, artistic books that contain a wider, richer vocabulary, the two viewpoints can be reconciled and the young child can enjoy the best of both worlds.

Information books

All children have a need to know, and information books of all types are needed to fulfil this basic need. Hundreds of books are published each year in all areas of art, science and social studies. There are also reference books, encyclopedias, handbooks and how-to-do-it books. The problem lies not in a shortage of information books, but rather in selecting those of quality.

Authors of information books for children must be extremely

knowledgeable in their particular field and also expert at putting complex concepts and terms into language young children can understand without having it sound watered down or condescending.

Used frequently, in appropriate ways, outstanding information books have the power to develop in young children a scientific mind, an inquiring outlook on life – an insatiable interest in finding out the how and why of things.

Children's books for language development: a basic collection

Mother Goose books

Book of Nursery and Mother Goose Rhymes compiled and illustrated by Marguerite de Angeli. Garden City, New York: Doubleday and Company, 1953

Brian Wildsmith's Mother Goose compiled and illustrated by Brian Wildsmith. New York: Franklin Watts, 1965

Mother Goose compiled and illustrated by Tasha Tudor. New York: Henry Z. Walck, 1944

The Real Mother Goose illustrated by Blanche Fisher Wright with introduction by May Hill Arbuthnot. Chicago: Rand McNally and Company, 1944

The Tall Book of Mother Goose compiled and illustrated by Feodor Rojankovsky. New York: Harper and Row, 1942

The Tenggren Mother Goose compiled and illustrated by Brian Wildsmith. New York: Franklin Watts, 1965

Alphabet books

ABC, An Alphabet Book photographed by Thomas Matthiesen. New York: Platt and Munk Publishers, 1966

First ABC written by Nancy Larrick and illustrated by Rene Martin. New York: Platt and Munk Publishers, 1965

In a Pumpkin Shell by Joan Walsh Anglund. New York: Harcourt Brace Jovanovich, 1960

The ABC Bunny by Wanda Gag. New York: Coward-McCann, 1933

The Marcel Marceau Alphabet Book written by George Mendoza and photographed by Milton H. Green. Garden City, New York: Doubleday and Company, 1970

Counting books

Ashanti to Zulu: African Traditions written by Margaret Musgrove and illustrated by Leo and Diane Dillon. New York: The Dial Press, 1976

Moja Means One: Swahili Counting Book written by Muriel Feelings and illustrated by Tom Feelings. New York: The Dial Press, 1971
My First Counting Book written by Lillian Moore and illustrated by Garth Williams. New York: Simon and Schuster, 1956
Still Another Number Book by Seymour Chwast and Martin Stephen Moskof. New York: McGraw-Hill Book Company, 1971
The Very Hungry Caterpillar by Eric Carle. Cleveland, Ohio: World Publishing Company, 1970
1 is One by Tasha Tudor. New York: Henry Z. Walck, 1956

Machines personified
Little Toot by Hardie Gramatky. New York: G. P. Putnam's Sons, 1939
Little Toot on the Thames by Hardie Gramatky. New York: G. P. Putnam's Sons, 1965
Little Toot Through the Golden Gate by Hardie Gramatky. New York: G. P. Putnam's Sons, 1975
Mike Mulligan and His Steam Shovel written and illustrated by Virginia Lee Burton. Boston: Houghton Mifflin Company, 1939
The Little Engine that Could by Watty Piper. New York: Platt and Munk Publishers, 1955

Concept books
Big Ones, Little Ones by Tana Hoban. New York: Macmillan, 1976
Fast-Slow, High-Low: A Book of Opposites by Peter Spier. New York: Doubleday and Company, 1972
Over, Under and Through by Tana Hoban. New York: Macmillan, 1973
The Adventures of Three Colors by Annette Tison and Talus Taylor. Cleveland, Ohio: World Publishing Company, 1971
We Read A to Z by Donald Crews. New York: Harper and Row, 1957

Humour and nonsense
Crictor by Tomi Ungerer. New York: Harper and Row, 1968
Horton Hatches the Egg by Dr Seuss (Theodor Seuss Geisel). New York: Random House, 1940
If All the Seas Were One Sea by Janina Domanska. New York: Macmillan, 1971
Johnny Crow's Garden by Leslie Brooke. New York: Frederick Warne and Company, 1903
Rain Makes Applesauce written by Julian Sheer and illustrated by Marvin Bileck. New York: Holiday House, 1964

Animal stories
Curious George by Hans A. Rey. Boston: Houghton Mifflin Company, 1941

Harry the Dirty Dog by Gene Zion. New York: Harper and Row, 1956
How, Hippo! by Marcia Brown. New York: Charles Scribner's Sons, 1969
The Little Rabbit Who Wanted Red Wings by Carolyn Sherwin Bailey. New York: Platt and Munk Publishers, 1951
The Secret Hiding Place by Rainey Bennett. Cleveland, Ohio: World Publishing Company, 1960

Picture books

Amigo written by Byrd Baylor Schweitzer and illustrated by Garth Williams. New York: Macmillan, 1963
Crow Boy by Taro Yashima. New York: The Viking Press, 1955
The Happy Owls by Celestino Piatti. New York: Atheneum, 1964
The Little Island written by Golden MacDonald and illustrated by Leonard Weisgard. Garden City, New York: Doubleday and Company, 1946
Time of Wonder by Robert McCloskey. New York: The Viking Press, 1957

Easy-to-read books

Are You My Mother? by P. D. Eastman. New York: Random House, 1960
Frog and Toad are Friends by Arnold Lobel. New York: Harper and Row, 1970.
Little Bear written by Else Holmelund Minarik and illustrated by Maurice Sendak. New York: Harper and Row, 1957
Little Bear's Friend written by Else Holmelund Minarik and illustrated by Maurice Sendak. New York: Harper and Row, 1961
Little Bear's Visit written by Else Holmelund Minarik and illustrated by Maurice Sendak. New York: Harper and Row, 1960

Information books

Seeds and More Seeds written by Millicent E. Selsam and illustrated by Tomi Ungerer. New York: Harper and Row, 1959
Soil by Richard Cromer. Chicago: Follett Publishing Company, 1967
What's Inside of Plants? by Herbert Zim. New York: William Morrow and Company, 1952
When an Animal Grows by Millicent Selsam. New York: Harper and Row, 1966
Your Friend, the Tree by Florence M. White. New York: Alfred A. Knopf, 1969

Part 3

Reading to learn

Reading to learn

Introduction

It seems to us that 'learning to read' and 'reading to learn' should be regarded as two aspects of one whole, almost like two sides of a coin. Although the process of learning to read must of necessity start before one can read to learn, there is a tremendous amount of overlap between the two. Children can learn through reading long before they have finished learning to read. It can be argued that during most of the years spent in school, say, from five to sixteen years, the two aspects of reading overlap to some extent.

The papers in this section have been selected with a view to reflecting the wide scope of the concept 'reading to learn', as we understand it. 'Reading to learn' is sometimes conceived in a rather narrow way – something like 'picking up factual information through reading'. This is certainly a very important aspect of reading to learn, and an aspect which is discussed by several of the contributors to this section. But it is only *one* aspect; many different kinds of things can be learned through reading. The outcomes of a reading act are, for example, seldom confined wholly to the cognitive domain. The affective domain is normally involved in one way or other. And in the reading of literature we are also reading to learn – not to learn facts and data, but to learn to understand people, society, ourselves, 'life', etc.

This section starts with a thought-provoking contribution by John Merritt, where he challenges some widespread, but perhaps not well-considered, notions about comprehension. His paper may not tell us what the 'rengles' do when they 'evimber' – he even leaves us in the dark as to the true nature of the 'Zobins' – but he forces us to think carefully about what is needed before we can say that we truly comprehend. It seems to us that John Merritt's curriculum for effective reading has far-reaching implications for the entire school curriculum. It can be regarded as a curriculum for thinking and for the building of knowledge.

The second paper also focuses on fundamental problems of reading comprehension. Sheila Harri-Augstein and Laurie Thomas may seem to suggest with their title 'Is comprehension the purpose of reading?' that the answer to that question is 'No'. This is not the case, however. What they suggest is rather that the traditional concept 'comprehension' is too narrow; that we must be concerned with how the purpose of reading affects comprehension. They also argue that this wider concept should be reflected in the way in which we assess comprehension.

The paper by Vera Southgate and her colleagues reports research results concerning a more practical, but certainly not less important, aspect of reading in our schools: the use of teachers' and children's time. Whatever our view of how reading skills should be developed, it seems reasonable to assume that a fair amount of time must be devoted to them. An analysis of how much time is spent on reading, and of how that time is used, is therefore very valuable.

Joyce Morris discusses some research evidence regarding how teacher attributes affect children's reading achievement. Despite the scarcity of relevant data, and despite some controversy about the interpretation of some of this data, she supports the Bullock Committee's conclusion that the quality and achievement of the teacher are of great importance.

The intriguing title 'Barking at Bullock' has been given to a paper which, in the authors' own words, reports 'an attempt to make a practical response to a practical problem'. The paper could also have been called 'Bullock at Barking', since it describes how the London Borough of Barking is attempting to implement one of the principal recommendations of the Bullock Report and to develop a 'systematic procedure for the prevention and treatment of learning difficulties'.

Jim Ewing's paper on attitudes brings to our attention the important affective domain in the field of reading. He emphasizes the fact that the cognitive and the affective domains are intertwined and must be studied jointly, and discusses in some detail various affective factors in reading – the main types of factors being 'reader factors' and 'situation factors'.

From a discussion of the affective aspects of reading we come naturally into the field of literature, to which the remaining three papers in this section are devoted. Jessie Reid's 'On becoming a reader' highlights the overlap between 'learning to read' and 'reading to learn'. A paper about becoming a reader would seem to belong under the heading 'Learning to read', and Jessie Reid does discuss various things which children must learn before they can become readers of literature. But in dealing with the role of literature, this paper also deals with one of the major uses of reading.

If the value of literature in the school curriculum can be taken for granted (and few would argue against it even if too little time time is devoted to it), there remains the question of *what* literature. It is a well-known fact that most children's books are bought by adults, so we should not be surprised if they are often selected on the basis of adult standards. In her contribution to this section, Margaret Spencer points out that literary criticism of children's books is mainly 'by adult standards', and argues that assessment should be more 'in the child's terms'.

If literature is sometimes neglected in a crowded junior- and secondary-school curriculum, one field of literature is often particularly neglected: namely poetry. The Bullock Report noted that poetry presents very special problems, and made some suggestions for their solutions. Norman Hidden develops arguments similar to those of the Bullock Committee, and emphasizes the need to bridge the generation gap by bringing truly contemporary poetry into the curriculum.

8 Learning to read and reading to learn: developing effective reading

John E. Merritt

For many teachers a child's reading comprehension is, in practice, little more than the ability to answer sets of questions thought up by the writer of a textbook, a reading workshop, or by the teacher herself. In this paper I will show how woefully inadequate a child's comprehension can be if his diet consists largely of such comprehension exercises. I will then consider three strategies which I believe are necessary for the development of effective reading. One of these strategies relates to the curriculum context within which we seek to develop effective reading. The second strategy is concerned with the way in which we encourage children to use all the cues a text provides as an aid to developing a fuller understanding of the individual words. The third strategy affects the way in which larger units of meaning may be organized by concentrating on the desired comprehension outcome.

What price comprehension?
How well do children actually comprehend what they read? How well do *you* comprehend what you read? Perhaps if we examine our own reading we might get a better idea of what we need to do to help our pupils. The text printed below, and the questions that follow, may help you to do this. As you read, try to imagine what it feels like to be a child presented with a textbook in which there are a number of unfamiliar words.

Comprehension processes
The *zobins* are usually *vimbole* – unlike most *rengles*. They often *evimber*, but not many of them do so in *grent*. Those that do are naturally *estingled*. Most *zobins glake slibdoms*, but if they use *dekinants* they normally *redintepone*. It takes a real *blegan* to *glake slibdoms*, although they are often thought to be *yive*.

Now you may think that you have not really understood very much from this passage because of the strange words that you encountered. In fact, I am going to show you that you have achieved a very considerable level of comprehension – if we are to place any reliance on typical comprehension questions. Indeed, the questions I shall set are not really very typical because they demand a much higher level of comprehension than is often demanded by the comprehension questions you find in textbooks –or in comprehension tests. Try these questions:

1 What is a *Zobin*?
2 What do *Zobins* do?
3 Which *Zobins* are not *estingled*?
4 Is it true what they say about *Zobins*?
5 How satisfactory is this text in terms of its presentation of ideas about *Zobins*?

First then: *What is a Zobin?* A *rengle*; a thing that is usually *vimbole*; a thing that often *evimbers*. This is a mere *literal* question – yet notice that the first answer was of a very high standard for it answered the question by providing a higher order classification, i.e. Zobins are a member of the more general class of 'rengle'. The other answers are also highly satisfactory for they represent the various attributes of the Zobin.

What do Zobins do? They usually *vimbole*; they often *evimber* (many of them do so in *grent*); they *glake slibdoms*; and if they use *dekinants* they normally *redintepone*. Here, the response to the question represents a certain degree of *reorganization* of the text. The literal question calls for a more or less thoughtful selection from what is actually in the text, whereas a reorganization question goes a stage further in demanding not just a simple selection but the extraction of a number of items which may then provide a summary, as in this case, a reclassification, or a synthesis of some kind.

Which Zobins are not estingled? There are some people whose minds go blank if they are presented with a mathematical problem in public. This question calls for a logical *inference* and I find it tends to have much the same effect. It is tempting here to say that all Zobins who do not evimber in grent are not estingled.

Logically, however, one cannot draw this conclusion, even though it looks rather plausible. It is certainly plausible enough for many casual readers to make this kind of inference even when they are reading texts in which all the words and ideas are very familiar.

Is it true what they say about Zobins? This question calls for some sort of *evaluation* process. For this kind of question, you would often draw upon your previous experience – although you cannot do so in this particular case. You might also check the text against other written sources, or against the observations of others. You might examine the text to see how much is fact and how much is opinion. In this particular case, one hopes you will reserve your judgment about Zobins unless you can find some internal inconsistency within the text which might in your view make a whole paragraph rather suspect. Certainly, however, you can consider the possibility of using a number of evaluation processes even though in this case your efforts are abortive and you have to reserve judgment.

How satisfactory is this text in terms of its presentation of ideas about Zobins? As the author of this rather strange text I hope you will spare me embarrassment by not answering this particular question, but I am sure that you will in fact have no difficulty in making such an *appreciation* – another aspect of the comprehension process.

At this stage, you will appreciate that you have engaged in all of the comprehension processes represented in the Barrett Taxonomy (see Clymer (1968)), and as I said earlier, this is a much more sophisticated series of questions than you are likely to find in most textbooks.

Yet in spite of your success – what do you actually comprehend about the Zobin? What this passage demonstrates is that you possess a tremendous linguistic facility. You have learned to answer questions in many subjects, and give the impression that you fully understand them, when all that you are doing in many cases is manipulating words. This is what we teach children to do for a large part of the time they spend in schools, and this is what they learn to do for a large part of their time even at college and university. Frankly, I think that throughout our schools, colleges, and universities, we are perpetuating mediocrity and semiliteracy through our failure to diagnose linguistic facility when it masquerades as comprehension. Indeed, I think we need first to diagnose ourselves because I am quite sure that we are quite often misled by our own linguistic competence into thinking that we understand what we are saying when in fact we understand as little about the particular topic as we do about the Zobin. It is only when we are really pressed by a critic who wants to achieve a much deeper level of comprehension that we begin to develop a real appreciation of our inadequacies. And the teacher or lecturer is rarely put in this position by a captive audience. Those who are linguistically competent learn to play the education game and duly glake their slibdoms. The others are all too often rejected by the teacher as being of modest intelligence and are then presented with an even more inferior diet.

A curriculum strategy

What this all means is that if we are concerned with reading comprehension we must start by thinking about the curriculum, for reading cannot be developed adequately unless we ensure that all students have an adequate range of concrete experiences to which they can relate what they read. Next, they will not develop the ability to process print effectively unless we ensure that each time they read they do so for a well-defined purpose – a purpose which has some immediate reality for them. And if we wish them to develop competence in reading the wide range of texts which they are likely to encounter in everyday life then we must give them experience of those kinds of texts during the school years.

The following lists give some indication of the kinds of printed texts adults encounter. The first list gives a very crude classification by format. The second list provides a starting-point for listing these various kinds of material in relation to the purposes for which they may be read within our various everyday life roles.

Texts and formats
Books
Fiction: novels, plays, anthologies.
Non-fiction: textbooks, monographs, biographies, autobiographies.

Periodicals
Journals, magazines, digests, etc.

Newspapers
Local – national, daily – weekly.

Regulations
Guarantees, insurance policies, credit agreements, employment contracts, by-laws, rules, constitutions.

Forms
Application forms: jobs, credit, insurance, clubs, etc.
Returns: income tax, census, car tax, etc.
Questionnaires: medical, political, psychological, etc.

Reference material
Catalogues, guides, quotations, invoices, statements, brochures, timetables, manuals, encyclopedia, dictionaries, abstracts, indexes, minutes, diaries, etc.

Correspondence
Letters, greetings, postcards, telegrams, invitations.
Official – personal, formal – informal.

Notices
Directions, labels, safety, store-signs, bus, indicators, facilities, traffic signs and symbols, etc.

Texts and roles
Home and family
School reports, circulars, health leaflets, rent books, insurance forms, cookery book, letters, postcards, invitations, DIY booklets, etc.

Employment
Job adverts, application forms, job particulars, T.U. literature, safety regulations, sick pay information, works notices, instruction manuals, etc.

Consumer
Advertising, labels, guarantees, credit agreements, discount house catalogues, etc.

Leisure

Sports news, travel brochures, holiday insurance forms, customs regulations, club rules, recurrent education literature, etc.

Community

Newspapers, political pamphlets, local government notices, community association literature, charity appeals, etc.

Clearly, however, there is no point in introducing income tax forms even to sixteen year olds. So what can we do? Somehow or other we have to introduce a wide range of role-purposes into the curriculum and help children to use materials which, if not identical to those of everyday life, are sufficiently closely related for them to serve as an effective introduction. For example, an activity that relates to the home and family role might be achieved by means of an investigation of school meals by children of almost any age. This might include the preparation of a questionnaire on preferences for completion by all the children in a class, an age group, or even a whole school. Both the preparation and the completion of the questionnaire can provide invaluable experience in judging how best to handle that particular type of text format – with all its potential uses and limitations. Similarly, the selection of school equipment, purchased by money raised through various functions, can provide an incentive to engage in the comprehension processes required of the intelligent consumer. Another starting-point for consumer reading might be some need that arises among the pupils themselves – an interest in stereo equipment, motor bikes, calculators, transistor radios or Christmas presents. Within the leisure role there is all the reading of tourist-agency literature – and, of course, geography textbooks – which can lead to the better selection of holiday venues. In addition, there are rules and regulations for the various games that children play, or watch on television, that could be more closely studied. Then there are surveys to be made of local leisure facilities and resource units to be developed for storing this information for regular access by the children themselves, by parents, or by visitors. And so one can go on.

It is not enough for people to say that we are educating children for life unless we take the trouble to examine all that life entails.

It is not enough to say that education consists of providing experiences that are most worthwhile here and now unless we can also demonstrate that they provide an *adequate* basis for the years that follow. Why must educational theorists argue as if these were alternatives? If we cannot achieve both goals then we are failing in our educational responsibilities. And it is only within the context of an effective curriculum that we can cater effectively for the development of reading comprehension.

A word comprehension strategy

Once we have begun to develop a more realistic curriculum we can turn our attention to the development of more effective teaching strategies. What kinds of teaching strategy are likely to help in developing reading comprehension?

First, it is quite obvious that comprehension cannot be developed effectively unless children have opportunities for enjoying practical experiences to which they can relate the verbal descriptions given by teachers and the various ideas they will encounter in textbooks or other literature. This does not mean, of course, that every single text is incomprehensible unless the reader has had the precise experience to which the text relates. If this were so, we could never enjoy a novel – and most textbooks would be almost incomprehensible. The important thing is that the reader should have a *sufficient* range of related experiences so that he can make reasonable inferences or extrapolations when he encounters an unknown word or an unfamiliar set of concepts. The following example gives you some idea of how this can happen.

The Prongies

The Duvals kept sheep, cows – and prongies. (1) The prongies were not kept for their wool or milk like the sheep and the cows, nor were they kept for their meat. But they did have to earn their keep. (2) Sure-footed, strong, and with considerable endurance, they did invaluable work in return for the food they ate. (3) The offspring of a male ass and a mare (4) is not an ideal beast of burden – but it has its uses.

In this passage I have deliberately included a range of different kinds of context cue. We would not normally expect to have so much assistance from context in any one paragraph. But when children meet a new word it then tends to crop up from time to time in different curriculum contexts and each time the child can learn a little more. This passage simply condenses this experience. If we look at it closely we can see how each type of cue can help the child to develop his understanding of new or unfamiliar words:

1 In the first sentence, the association of prongies with two other words in the form of a list would normally suggest that they all have something in common, i.e. we have a *class membership* cue. In this particular case, the dash suggests that although prongies bear some relationship to sheep and cows they may also perhaps be different in certain ways.

2 In the next two sentences, certain attributes of sheep and cows are listed and this provides a *comparison* or *contrast* cue. The reader can now modify his or her hypothesis about what prongies are – or are not. This, incidentally, confirms our original suspicion that there may be two animals. But are prongies animals? They might even be tractors! Or Land Rovers!

3 Here, we are given certain direct information about prongies – an *attributes* cue. We now know something about what prongies are like – not just what they are not like.

4 Finally, we are given a definition which enables us to define prongies as a class of animal produced by the mating of a male ass with a mare – a *category* cue. (The remainder of the sentence gives an additional *attributes* cue.)

All context cues do not fit perfectly into the above categories. An analysis of this kind does provide a useful starting-point, however, and it may be helpful for some children to be made aware of the nature of these different kinds of cue.

As we tend to encounter words in different contexts, it is particularly important that we should derive the maximum amount of meaning from each specific context, as false impressions set up on one occasion can all too easily lead to misinterpretation when the unfamiliar word crops up in subsequent contexts. For example, we might well have thought that prongies were dogs, perhaps, or horses. Unless we have a very open mind this impression could easily be confirmed by all the other cues except the final category cue. Often, however, we may not encounter an obvious category cue – or we may meet it in a context where it is easy to assume that it refers to something else. Indeed, even in the above text, a poor reader struggling at what is for him instructional or even frustration level, might well have forgotten all about prongies by the time he got to the end of the paragraph. If he assumed that a prongie was a horse then he might take it for granted that the last sentence refers to another animal altogether! This testifies to the folly of encouraging children to read aloud without paying *scrupulous* attention to meaning.

In order to ensure that a child does pay scrupulous attention to meaning, however, we have to be sure that the child has a genuine reading purpose and is not merely reading in order to demonstrate his prowess in barking at words.

In addition to ensuring that all reading is purpose-directed we must naturally give children certain kinds of assistance. In the first sentence, for example, we could invite children to make a list of those attributes of sheep and cows which they suspect might be significant in this particular context. They might then be invited to hypothesize about which attributes are shared by prongies – and which might be different. It is important to do this before reading on, for otherwise children would simply learn to read in an uncritical and sloppy fashion instead of making best use of the information that is readily available. If the comparison–contrast cue occurred soon afterwards, they could then check off those items which agreed with their hypothesis and which of their ideas were incorrect. In another text they might perhaps pick up additional attributes. Children who get hooked on this kind of problem-solving approach would then be more likely, in my view, to spot a category cue such as that provided in the last sentence of the above text.

Everything, you will notice, hangs on the question of whether or not the children are really genuinely interested and not just playing the game of 'please the teacher'. When we teach children to read material in which they are not really interested we do more harm than good. It is not just that we are neglecting comprehension – the problem is that we are positively training them in mindless reading. Given such training, plus lack of motivation, we have a sure recipe for underachievement.

In presenting this argument I am often told that the children should simply look in the dictionary. The limitation of this approach is well demonstrated by Robinson (1976). He quotes the case of a teacher of English who asked children to look up the word 'trite' in the dictionary and to write a sentence to demonstrate its meaning. They produced the following responses:

The miners who have gone on strike are trite. (trite = 'overworked')
This bread is trite. (trite = 'worn out')
The shoes I am wearing are trite. (trite = 'worn out')

The trouble is that all words have multiple meanings, or many shades of meaning. In fact, according to Fries (1963) the most frequent 500 words in the English language share between them 14,050 meanings – an average of twenty-nine meanings per word. This problem is illustrated in the following examples using everyday words and everyday meanings:

1 It is a fast car.
   It is a fast day.
   She is a fast cat.
   It is a fast colour.

2 Push it up the bank.
   Put it in the bank.
   Don't bank to the left.
   Don't bank on it.

3 He is a mean individual.
   That is the mean temperature.
   Did he mean to do that?
   Did he mean 'yes'?

In the first part of this paper I mentioned that many ideas are presented in such a way that it is almost impossible to derive meaning. On the other hand, I have shown that a great deal of meaning can be derived from texts – provided that the reader has sufficient experience in making full and effective use of the cues that are available. That is what we have got to do in our teaching –and this is the message that we have got to get across to our colleagues who teach in the various subject areas.

A comprehension outcome strategy

It is not enough simply to help children to use context cues in order to identify word meanings. We must also help them to comprehend larger units of meaning. Here, I would argue that comprehension does not consist of converting words into other sets of words.

Rather, it consists of recognizing relationships. If, for example, a text describes a physical or geographical feature, then the reader must comprehend the spatial relationships between the various parts. A measure of his understanding would be his ability to reproduce an accurate diagram of the object, or a map. When classes of objects are described it may be that comprehension can best be demonstrated by a drawing which represents each class member as an item in a set, or an intersection. If various attributes are given for each class member, as in the case of sheep, cows and prongies, comprehension could be demonstrated by listing the attributes along one axis of a table and the categories along the other axis. Ticks in each cell can be used to show which member has which attribute and these ticks provide a simple means of making comparisons or contrasts. This is a particularly useful device where it is necessary, for some reason, to sort out subcategories, as in the example given in Table 1.

Table 1 Mammals and reptiles

	viviparous	lays eggs	suckles young	does not suckle young	warm blooded	cold blooded	has hair	has scales
Mammals								
Cow	✓		✓		✓		✓	
Dog	✓		✓		✓		✓	
Horse	✓		✓		✓		✓	
Mouse	✓		✓		✓		✓	
Platypus		✓	✓		✓		✓	
Reptiles								
Turtle		✓		✓		✓		✓
Snake		✓		✓		✓		✓
Crocodile		✓		✓		✓		✓
Lizard		✓		✓		✓		✓

In the next example, taken from Merritt (1975), flow diagrams provide a convenient format for demonstrating a pattern of trading relationships and an attributes matrix provides a means of comparing markets and fairs (see also The Open University 1977).

Merchants of Venice
The goods brought from the Far East to Venice did not of course remain in Venice. They were taken to all parts of Europe to be sold. Venetian merchants came to England to visit the fairs that were held in the largest towns of the country once or twice a year. Markets, which were less important than fairs, since they were for local needs, were held weekly in almost every town.

Model 1

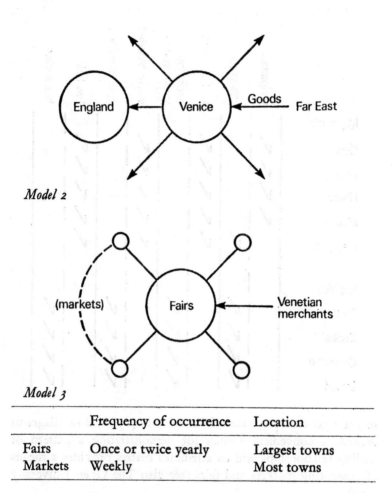

Model 2

Model 3

	Frequency of occurrence	Location
Fairs	Once or twice yearly	Largest towns
Markets	Weekly	Most towns

If you take the trouble to compare each element in the above models with the related items in the text you will notice that the models are less than perfect. In fact, there is one major inaccuracy. Notice, too, that although certain elements are derived from 'reading the lines', others are the product of 'reading between the lines' and even 'beyond the lines' (Gray (1960)). From normal, careful reading you will be able to decide which inferences and extrapolations were legitimate and which were not.

You will also appreciate that each illustration provides a

springboard for further thought. Imagine, for example, what it might mean in the first model if arrows were drawn going in the opposite direction; or imagine what an extra row or column might represent in model 3.

Now the point about asking children to produce reading outcomes of this kind is that it helps to make at least part of their comprehension explicit. It gives you a chance to help the child to check his comprehension carefully in an almost mathematical way. At the same time, it provides a starting-point for discussion. No less important, perhaps, it provides you with a valuable diagnostic instrument which you can use quite informally in your teaching – either taking up issues on the spot, or filing them in memory for another occasion.

I know many of you will already have used many of the ideas expressed in this paper at one time or another. What I am arguing here is that we must be much more rigorous and systematic in using the kinds of strategy I have described. I do not mean by this that we should set up artificial exercises each day and timetable boring sessions for text analysis. What I do mean is that we should be careful not to miss the many opportunities that arise each day for encouraging children to read purposefully, and to make much fuller use of the rich variety of cues in all the texts they read. Remember, the more time they spend reading passively the more they will tend to develop the habit of reading in this way. And it is not just our own teaching that we must watch. It is equally important that we awake our colleagues to the dangers – and the opportunities. If we succeed, we shall have made a significant contribution to education.

References

CLYMER, T. (1968) 'What is reading?: some current concepts' in A. Melnik and J. Merritt (eds) Reading: Today and Tomorrow University of London Press/The Open University Press

FRIES, C. C. (1963) Linguistics and Reading New York: Holt, Rinehart and Winston

GRAY, W. S. (1960) 'The major aspects of reading' in H. M. Robinson (ed.) Sequential Development of Reading Abilities Supplementary Educational Monographs No. 90. Chicago: University of Chicago Press

MERRITT, J. E. (1975) Reading: seven to eleven Education 3–13 2, 1

ROBINSON, H. A. (1976) *Teaching Reading and Study Strategies: The Content Areas* Allyn and Bacon

THE OPEN UNIVERSITY (1977) 'Developing independence in reading' in PE231 *Reading Development* Block 2, Units 5, 6, 7 and 8. The Open University Press

9 Is comprehension the purpose of reading?

Sheila Harri-Augstein and Laurie F. Thomas

Comprehension in reading can be considered as a process of sampling, searching and selecting the hieroglyphics on a page in order to attribute meaning to them. Different purposes of reading and different ways of processing the linear strings of words, sentences and paragraphs enable individuals to attribute a wide variety of meaning to the same text. This eyeball-to-print interaction, whereby personal meaning is generated, has not been given the attention it merits in the curricula of our primary and secondary schools. The Bullock Report alerts us to this and recommends the implementation of comprehensive programmes for developing competence in reading comprehension throughout a child's school life.

That our educational system has failed to provide an effective programme for encouraging reading competency is evident all around us. Students at colleges of higher education complain that they are disadvantaged by their ineffective reading skills and confess that they cannot cope with the vast resource of print which is a major part of their learning diet. Thousands of illiterate adults of average and above average IQ cope by developing avoidance strategies, thus hiding their disability. Others have become alienated from the 'print society' and have opted out. Many professionals in a wide variety of employment situations feel the need to improve their reading skills. Commerical courses capitalize on this need, but a comprehensive survey of the programmes they offer shows the narrow terms in which competent performance is defined (Pugh 1974). Emphasis is given to speed at the expense of comprehension in a wider sense.

Why has the effective development of reading competence been inadequate in the classroom? In general, it can be said that neither the technology nor the theoretical framework within which reading-for-learning could be adequately taught has been available. Despite the wealth of literature on the topic, the psychological data available is too inadequate and therefore there is no basis on which to develop a valid, reliable comprehensive model of the reading process. In the absence of such a model, no systematic programme for effecting change and improvement in competency is possible. What we have is, at best, a series of pragmatic, partial approaches. At worst, we have completely ignored the problem.

Throughout our educational institutions emphasis has been given to the product of comprehension, rather than to the process of comprehending. The criteria against which the teacher evaluates the product of the reader's comprehension may not be those which the reader himself uses when he is comprehending. When a teacher indicates that a pupil has failed, that pupil may in reality have successfully tackled a different task. The fact that the task appears trivial or bizarre does not allow us to avoid the implications. Individual learners interpret a reading assignment in uniquely different ways. Despite the best of intentions, teachers cannot get into the learner's head; they cannot predict exactly how the learner interprets a particular reading task, except in the very simplest fact-finding exercises. Not only is this the case, but most learners are not aware of their own intentions, nor how they propose to implement these. They may, in very general terms, say that they are reading 'to understand', or say that they are going to 'skip through once' and then 'go through carefully', but beyond this very crude level of process description, they are blind.

In our research we have found that a useful approach to this dilemma is to consider comprehension as part of the process of learning.

Comprehension as learning

Jahoda and Thomas (1966) have distinguished three types of learning. *Type A learning* is the inference made by the teacher in terms of what he expects the learner to learn. Almost all academic learning is defined in this way. Reading-comprehension tests assess what it is that the teacher, experimenter, or test designer thinks the reader should learn from the text. In order to be systematic, tests incorporate items which are unambiguous and easy to mark. This degrades the process of comprehension into a fairly mundane fact-finding activity. There are a variety of taxonomies of learning (e.g. Bloom, Barrett, Gagné and Melton), all of which assume a Type A stance, but even within this restricted view the measures of comprehension occupy only a small segment of the total set of alternatives which individuals are capable of generating.

Type B learning is inferred from the learner's point of view. It poses a rather more difficult problem of assessment. Prior to the activity, the learner cannot know the content of the material that he is setting out to learn and cannot, therefore, prospectively design a test which would adequately assess how well he has achieved his purpose. Often the position of the teacher and the learner changes as a result of the teaching/learning process and their view of the purpose and criteria for assessment is consequently adjusted.

Type C learning is an inference made retrospectively in the light of the learning experience, when both purpose and outcome can be fully articulated. In practice this presents difficulty of assessment within the traditional framework. The classical essay-type or free-response question is obviously designed to meet this more open-ended learning experience. But hidden between the lines lies a wealth of personal-meaning attribution, which is very often never recognized by the teacher, however hard he tries to enter into a Type C type of assessment. The only way out of this dilemma is for the teacher and learner to work together creating an encounter whereby the dynamic development of purpose and the criteria for the evaluation of the process of meaning attribution can be made explicit. The difficulties involved in designing tests which measure the quality of individual reading comprehension as well as the universal lack of procedures for a combined teacher/learner negotiation within a Type C framework explain why, in practice, teachers revert over and over again to the Type A approach.

Type A definitions mix two different problems of learning. If the learner is skilled but is pursuing a purpose which is radically different from that of the teacher, the teacher's assessment of what he is doing may indicate a very poor learning performance. If the teacher then infers that the learner is unskilled and feeds this back to the learner, he or she may become alienated and disgruntled, because his problem is not one of skill but one of negotiating the similarities and differences between the directions in which the teacher wants to go and the directions in which he wants to go of his own accord. Comprehending is understanding and understanding is essentially a question of coming to grips with a topic in one's own terms. There is obviously a question of how well those terms map on to the intentions of the teacher or the institution, but that is a separate question – it's a question of purpose, loyalty and clarification of one's vocational or educational directions. It's certainly not a question of comprehending.

How, then, are we to approach the problem of helping children and adults to develop their own capacity to learn and thus the process of reading for comprehension?

Reading for learning
Readers fail to become effective versatile learners for three basic reasons:

1 They are unable to formulate adequate operational purposes and therefore read in a rather vaguely orientated or nonspecific way.

2 They are unaware of the ways in which they read. At best they have a crude idea of sometimes skimming or scanning, sometimes reading carefully and sometimes going back and looking at something. But most people are unable to control this and believe that the process of reading happens to them as they get at the meaning in the text, rather than being something which they can develop and use as a versatile learning skill.

3 They are unable to assess the quality of the learning outcome which is achieved during reading. Most readers will give only very vague and evasive answers if asked what exactly they have learnt when they put down a book. The whole question of understanding and being able to assess personally one's own learning outcomes is hardly ever examined in the educational situation. The whole process of assessment is handed over to the teacher and the learner becomes a closely-supervised worker at the task of extracting meaning from, or attributing meaning to, the text.

The effective reader for learning is able to articulate a wide variety of different purposes and is able to draw on a wide variety of different strategies and tactics in reading. He is also able to assess his learning outcomes in a wide variety of ways and he is capable of being aware of any or all of these processes at the various levels of interaction with a text – from words, through sentences, to paragraphs, to the whole meaning of an article. He is, in fact, an expert at controlling the whole process of learning by reading.

The Centre for the Study of Human Learning has, over a period of years, developed a variety of tools and a conversational methodology for approaching this problem of helping people to learn to read-for-learning, i.e. for exploring the process of comprehending.

First, a simple Reading Recorder was developed (Harri-Augstein and Thomas 1973). It enables the reader to see exactly how he has moved his eyes over the text. It shows him where he hesitates and the rate at which he is reading; it shows his change of pace, where he goes back or skips forward. It maps out on an almost line-by-line basis exactly how the reader has spent his time in interacting with the black hieroglyphics on the page.

Having found that the reading process could be recorded, and a reader's strategies identified (Thomas and Harri-Augstein 1972), the next question was how to assess the outcomes of reading. A Flow Diagram Technique was developed in which the 'structure of meaning' in the text could be expressed (Thomas 1974). It was important to separate the meaning of a text from the syntactic structure of the sentences. By assigning categories such as 'Main ideas', 'Qualifiers' and 'Elaborators', and by numbering the 'Meaning items' in a text, it becomes possible to classify each item and show by means of arrows the relationships between them. To begin with, a panel of experts examined the text in detail and mapped out how meaning ran through the paragraphs and the sentences on the page. However, as we began to use this technique two things became clear. First, experts can comprehend different meanings from the same text, differing in their views about exactly what the meaning structure of a text might be. Second, we began to realize that the Flow Diagram Technique was a very useful way of expressing what had been understood whilst reading. Thus, from being a multi-dimensional way of describing the 'literal' meaning of the text, we recognized that it was a way of describing the personal meaning that one has attributed to it. Having made this subjective jump, it was realized that the Flow Diagram Technique was in itself a way of expressing what had been comprehended. It can be used to represent the pattern of meanings in a person's head in a visual articulated form. Thus, separated from the meaning-attributing process, one could stand back and review it in terms of how well it expressed the successful outcome to one's purpose.

Having thus been able to record the process of reading and externalize the outcomes of reading expressed in personal terms, it was possible to begin to examine how strategies and outcomes relate one to another. The results were interesting. Some people have very little idea of how strategy relates to purpose, others have more explicit assumptions, but are unable to assess their own success in realistic terms. Gradually it became apparent that meaning was best understood in relativistic terms and that comprehension is a process of negotiation between the reader and the text, whereby structures of meaning are created in his head.

At this phase in the research programme, it was realized that whilst the combination of the Flow Diagram Technique and the Reading Recorder was extremely powerful for sharpening awareness of the process of reading-for-learning, there were also serious limitations. The display of a reader's attribution of meaning by means of a Flow Diagram confines the reader too closely to the text, and inhibits the exploration of the reader's own ideas. The read record must be linked to the reader's purpose and his criteria for assessing the quality of the outcome in order to be meaningful in a Type C learning framework. It needed, therefore, to be combined with a personally-orientated open-ended tool designed to capture fully the process of individual meaning attribution. This entailed the development of procedures for displaying 'structures of meaning' which a reader generates during the eyeball-to-print interaction.

Tool for measuring Type C learning
The problem with assessing the 'structures of meaning' which are generated during reading is that they first occur in the head and

gut. In this whole-self activity, the outcome is some change in the reader's thoughts and feelings. This becomes represented in the reader's store of uniquely personal knowing. Except in the most formal reading, the reader is only partially aware of the range and richness of the 'structures of meaning' he generates. Even if he attends to it, he experiences great difficulty in reconstructing the fullness of the reading event unaided. Left in his head, it is easy for the reader to delude himself, believing that his understanding was better, or worse, than it actually was.

How can the 'structures of meaning' be externalized, so that a more systematic review becomes possible? This must be achieved sensitively and rigorously with the minimum of 'pollution' from others' heads. The development of a tool to meet this requirement represents an important move away from standardized tests, criterion-referenced tests and informal teacher tests, which measure Type A learning. Such tests are more concerned with selection and prediction of abilities and are for teacher diagnosis rather than learner diagnosis. A Type C tool for measuring learner-based comprehension becomes an essential instrument for individually based, informal reading inventories (IRI) which are currently being introduced into the schools' curriculum.

The procedure for the visual representation of 'structures of meaning' involves:

1 eliciting items of meaning
2 defining the relationship between items
3 displaying the pattern.

This different approach to express meaning, in contrast with essays and other linear expositions, pulls the reader out of a fixed acceptance of ideas in language and challenges him to think anew. Aided by the teacher/tutor, the reader becomes more aware of the complexity of structure in even the simplest meanings.

The procedure can be summarized briefly as follows. A more detailed algorithm is available for further reference (Thomas and Harri-Augstein 1974).

Eliciting the items of meaning: step one
Having read the text, various techniques from free association,

oblique and bizarre associations, divergent, convergent and deductive thinking and brain storming, can be recruited by the reader and teacher to generate 'items of meaning'. The choice of elicitation technique depends on the person, the purpose and the text. 'Trying to remember' is simply not enough. Type A learning experiences lead to the development of intuitive, almost automatic internal checking processes, which suppress many potential thoughts. Learners are cut off from much of their own internal resources. This is true at the direct-recall level and the more wider-ranging level that is the basis of creative work – the greater the repertoire of techniques for eliciting items, the greater the accessing possibilities into the potentially rich internal resource. The items of meaning elicited define the 'universe of discourse' within which dimensions of meaning can be constructed.

Defining the relationships between the items: step two
By comparing every item with every other item, or by successive sorting of the items or by using pre-set categories, relationships can be drawn between the items. In asking 'what goes with what', various dimensions of pattern emerge.

Displaying the pattern: step three
Different display techniques illustrate the various ways in which 'structures of meaning' can be made explicit. Again, the choice of technique is influenced by the reader's purpose and text. One way of drawing up a structure is in the form of a 'Meaning Net'. A net of items will show how items of meaning cluster into distinct patterns of meaning. Nodes of meaning focus the dimensions of thought within the structure. Such nodes can be categorized so that the node represents an item of meaning at another level of the hierarchy of structure. The relationships between the nodes can also be specified.

Once the items of meaning and the relationships between them are made explicit, in the form of a visual display, the reader alone, or the reader and teacher together, can begin to review the process of meaning attribution. How does the 'structure of meaning' relate to the purpose of reading? How does it relate to strategy? Does it reflect any mismatch between the reader's original purpose and a retrospectively defined purpose? How well does the struc-

Figure 1 An algorithm for displaying and assessing structures of meaning

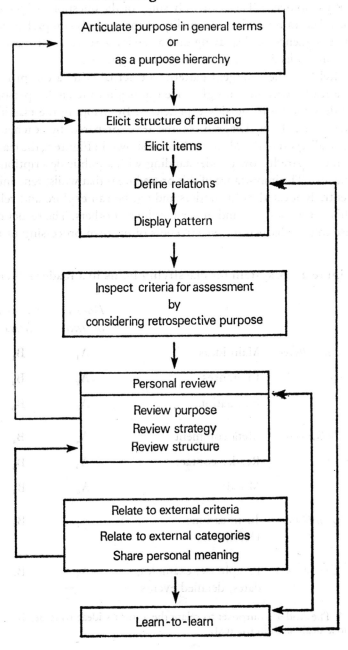

ture reflect the reader's purpose? Would a further sampling of the text produce a better outcome; if so, what tactics would be usefully employed? These are only some of the questions which can be asked in reviewing the quality of the reader's comprehension. The sequence of displaying and assessing structures of meaning is summarized in the Flow Diagram (Figure 1).

Relating the emergent pattern to external criteria can provide the reader with new insights. He can begin to relate his personal understanding to outside experiences. By mapping the classified items in a Flow Diagram of the text (prepared by teacher or specialist) on to the Meaning Net, as shown in Figure 2, the reader can compare his own understanding with a public description of the text. The importance of this procedure is that whilst remaining centrally located in his understanding, he can explore and relate this to the thoughts and understandings of others. The reader can use this to sharpen the effectiveness of his own processing of the

Figure 2   A system for classifying items in a reader's Net*

		Items in the text	*Imagined items*
Main theme	Main ideas	A_1	B_1
	Inferences	A_2	B_2
	Evaluations	A_3	B_3
Indications	Meta-comment	A_4	B_4
	Reader contact	A_5	B_5
	Mood	A_6	B_6
Qualifications	Justifications Definitions	A_7	B_7
Elaborations	Paraphrase, examples, dates, detailed events	A_8	B_8

* The reader's purpose: to relate the author's ideas to issues beyond those dealt with in the text.

text. Any mismatch between his own purpose and outcome will be revealed by an examination of his pattern in the light of the introduced categories. Can the items in the Net be traced back to the text? If not, do they contribute to his own comprehension in some way? If his purpose can be defined as extrapolating from the author's own ideas, then he should expect to find more B than A items in the Net. If, on the other hand, his intention was to summarize the text, A_1, A_2 and A_3 items should predominate.

Another way in which the reader can relate his personal understanding to outside experiences is to share his Net with others. Two or more individuals – peer learners, learner and tutor, teacher and a group of learners – can agree to share a purpose, read the same text and each can display his 'structure of meaning' in the form of a Net. This sharing process depends on specific procedures for ensuring a creative encounter whereby each participant gains new insights and personal meaning is restructured. These are described elsewhere (see Harri-Augstein and Thomas 1976).

Learning-to-learn

Human beings have an infinite capacity for generating new structures of meaning through their acts of construction on the world, reading being one special case. The elicitation of these structures in the form of visible displays opens up a wide range of learning experiences. The displays act as a 'mirror'. In contemplating this reflection of personal meaning, the learner becomes more aware of the richness of the meaning in his head. The mirror reflects the learner's own process and he can use this 'psycho-feedback' for developing his own language about learning. He is acting as a 'scientist', observing and interpreting his own learning. The science is that of learning-to-learn.

The learner can explore how structures of meaning are constructed, how past experience, values and beliefs, needs and purposes, as well as strategies and tactics, all contribute to these constructions. 'Purpose', 'strategy' and 'outcome' provide the context within which structures of meaning can be evaluated. He thus learns to review his learning competency.

The self-organized learner is in a better position to learn effectively from future interactions with his world, with other people, events and things. Not only by reading can he practise his self-organized approach to learning, but also by listening, writing, discussing and doing. Our experience is that he cannot achieve this unaided. But by getting into a 'conversation' with his tutor in ways which enable him to experience Type C learning, he rapidly learns to internalize the dialogues which foster learning-to-learn (Harri-Augstein and Thomas, in press).

In educational practice such creative encounters depend on the flair and intuitive skills of a few gifted teachers. In action-research projects carried out in schools, colleges of higher education and industry, the techniques described in this paper and others reported elsewhere (Thomas *et al.* 1976) have been employed for the rigorous analysis and systemization of Type C learning interactions. A conversational methodology has been developed and a science of Learning Conversations has been formulated (Harri-Augstein and Thomas, in press). Such 'conversations' are controlled, purposeful and highly skilled. In the early stages, the responsibility lies almost entirely with the tutor, who initiates and monitors the 'conversational events'. These depend on the use of awareness-raising tools and procedures for reflecting the learning process back to the learner. With the help of personal support and sustained guidance, the learner gradually moves towards greater self-organization as he or she develops competence in controlling the Learning Conversation. The learner becomes his or her own tutor.

Reading as a Learning Conversation: Type C comprehension
It is useful to consider the process of reading as a Learning Conversation between the individual and the text. To be more precise, the conversation goes on in the reader's head and gut. One participant in the conversation stays closely with the sequence of words on the page (literal comprehension), the other takes off imaginatively from the words, intuitively interpreting, criticizing, analysing and extrapolating (higher levels of comprehension). The interaction between these two components in the conversation is the essence of comprehension. Extreme inbalance in either direction can produce one or other of the kinds of malaise from which we, the products of our educational system, suffer, either as over-conformist or as undisciplined thinkers. Within this conversa-

tional framework *Type A Learning* can be seen as leading to '*Type A Comprehension*' and to conformist thinking. This is what reading tests measure, but reading-for-learning is about more. If comprehension is about what reading achieves, then it is *Type C Comprehension*, where the terms for assessing meaning are negotiated with the learner. Type C Comprehension frees the learner so that, aided 'conversationally' by his tutor, he can develop his self-organizing capacity and reading-for-learning competency.

References

AUGSTEIN, E. S. HARRI- and THOMAS, L. F. (1973) *Developing your own Reading* The Open University Press
AUGSTEIN, E. S. HARRI- and THOMAS, L. F. (1976) 'Zen and the art of getting a Degree'. Monograph for Brunel students. Centre for the Study of Human Learning, Brunel University
AUGSTEIN, E. S. HARRI- and THOMAS, L. F. (in press) 'Towards a theory of learning conversation and a paradigm for conversational research' in M. Howe (Ed) *Recent Research in Adult Learning* (provisional title) Wiley
JAHODA, M. and THOMAS, L. F. (1966) The mechanics of learning *New Scientist* 14, April
PUGH, A. K. (1974) 'The design and evaluation of reading efficiency courses'. M. Phil. thesis. University of Leeds
THOMAS, L. F. (1974) 'The flow diagram technique'. Centre for the Study of Human Learning, Brunel University
THOMAS, L. F. *et al* (1976) Technical Reports 1–100. Centre for the Study of Human Learning, Brunel University. Publications list on request.
THOMAS, L. F. and AUGSTEIN, E. S. HARRI- (1972) An experimental approach to the study of reading as a learning skill *Research in Education* 8
THOMAS, L. F. and AUGSTEIN, E. S. HARRI- (1974) 'A structures of meaning kit'. Centre for the Study of Human Learning, Brunel University

10   The use of teachers' and children's time in *Extending Beginning Reading*

Vera Southgate, Helen Arnold and Sandra Johnson

Introduction

The Schools Council Project *Extending Beginning Reading* lasted for four years, 1973-7 and an outline of the research in progress was presented to the twelfth annual conference of UKRA in 1975 (Southgate 1976). The project was concerned with average readers in the first two years of 'junior education', i.e. children aged 7+ to 9+, who had mastered the 'beginning reading' stage. The main aims of the project were:

to discover exact details of these children's competencies and the ways in which they utilized their reading skills

to locate points at which difficulties occurred and the strategies the children employed to overcome these difficulties

to note the methods their teachers used to help the children to 'extend' their proficiency, as well as the progress the children made during these two years of schooling; and

to examine, in the children, habits and attitudes likely to ensure the full utilization of their reading abilities outside school.

During the first two years of the project, the research team, in addition to working with large Teachers' Reading Research Groups, followed a programme of preliminary investigations in twenty schools drawn from five LEAs, which brought them into close contact with some 750 children and their teachers. These two complementary aspects of the research programme led to the development of appropriate techniques for use in a more detailed study, in depth, of a small number of schools in the third year of the project. They culminated in a pilot study carried out in three schools, in which the assessments, questionnaires, interviews, records and observation schedules which had been developed for use in the 'intensive study' were tried out.

The intensive study year

The aim of the 'intensive study' was to obtain, by means of a diverse battery of probing techniques, an accurate and detailed picture of all those processes affecting children learning to read, and using their reading abilities, which are day-to-day occurrences in typical junior classrooms.

The intensive study was concerned throughout the year with thirty-four first- and second-year junior classes in twelve schools in four LEAS which could be regarded as 'typical'. Small 'remedial' classes were not used. A large number of probing techniques were employed in the schools during the year, including a variety of assessments, interviews and observations. Certain of the measures concerned every child in these classes, whereas others were used with only four children who had been randomly selected from the band of children of average reading ability in each class.

This particular paper refers to only one of the methods of investigation employed in the intensive study year, namely the use of classroom observation schedules. Moreover, the facts presented are limited to only one feature of the tentative findings emerging from a preliminary analysis of the observation schedules – the use of teachers' and pupils' time. Additional information about this and other aspects of the observation schedules will be included in the final report of the project.

Classroom observation techniques

A number of British researchers have conducted observational studies of teachers' and/or children's classroom behaviour in junior schools: for example, Hilsum and Cane (1971), Resnick (1972), Garner and Bing (1973) and Boydell (1974 and 1975). However, the researchers in the project *Extending Beginning Reading* have failed to discover reports of exercises involving specifically reading and writing activities in English junior classes. The observation schedules used in this research project were, therefore, devised for this purpose.

After extensive trials and revisions, two observation schedules, one referring to the teacher and one to the pupil, were finally produced. The schedules were intended to be used in normal class situations, and were designed as records of all those activities

E

connected with reading and writing engaged in by the individual under observation. A time-sampling technique involving the recording of behaviour at thirty-second intervals was employed and a portable cassette recorder was used as a timekeeper.

Tables 1 (a) and 1 (b): Behaviour categories in observation schedules

Table 1 (a) – Teacher categories
1 Gives direct instructions related to reading or writing.
2 Recounts or reads from a book.
3 Explains or expands book content.
4 Organizes or supervises reading or writing activity.
5 Listens to oral reading.
6 Supplies a word or spelling.
7 Directs copying or literal recall.
8 Requires pupils' ideas on reading or writing.
9 Comments on reading or writing activity, i.e. provides feedback.
10 Engaged in other teaching activity – not related to reading or writing.
11 Engaged in activities not directly related to teaching behaviour.

Table 1 (b) – Child categories
1 Listens to teacher (or media) reading or giving instruction in reading.
2 Listens to another child reading.
3 Reads assigned book.
4 Reads self-selected book.
5 Writes, while referring to a book or other printed materials.
6 Writes without reference to book or other materials.
7 Engaged in other tasks where reading or writing is not involved.
8 Asks a question about reading or writing activity.
9 Answers a question on reading or writing activity.
10 Volunteers an answer.
11 Spontaneous contribution on reading or writing activity.
12 Non-orientated activity.

Both schedules made provision for a brief description of the lesson with a record of the type of organization and the reading materials in use at every stage. In addition, the teacher's schedule provided for recording each occasion on which the teacher switched attention from one child or group to another, and also for noting the size of the group with which she was engaged.

Using the observation schedules

The observers used in the classroom observation study were either B.Ed. students in their final year at a college of education or practising teachers following a university diploma course. Two training sessions using videotape recordings were followed by two 'live' practice sessions in classrooms.

The actual observation study took place during the autumn and spring terms, individual sessions lasting twenty minutes. Although thirty observers were involved at the various stages of the study, the majority of observations were made by fourteen of these. Usually two observers worked together in a classroom, with one recording the teacher's behaviour while the other observed the child. The child in question was unaware that he or she was being observed. Although the teacher knew that she might be under observation, she was never sure whether she was being observed in a particular session or not, and so learned very quickly to ignore the observers.

Observations were undertaken in five schools, and, whenever possible, were confined to periods concerned with reading and writing activities. The following figures refer solely to such sessions. One hundred and twenty-eight observation sessions were recorded for twenty teachers, the number per teacher varying between three and nine; and 195 records were made for a total of sixty-eight children, the number per child varying from one to eight.

Preliminary findings

Time spent on reading/writing activities – in general
The observation record sheets show up fascinating patterns of what the teacher and child really do when reading and writing periods are in progress. What comes out very clearly is how hard

the teachers work. Even so, the records indicate that the teacher does not always do what she thinks she is doing, nor is the child always doing what the teacher thinks he is doing.

The first general point to note is that the actual total time devoted to reading and writing activities was considerably less than most teachers imagined it to be. Teachers might think, for instance, that a session of reading and/or writing is included in every day's programme. But reading or writing lessons were not always taking place. The reasons for the changes were varied. For example, the class might be preparing for a concert or harvest festival, some children might be going on an outing, or a policeman might have visited the school to talk about road safety. The result was that the teacher's aims and objectives for the term, which they had written out in advance, may not have been fully implemented because the total time spent on reading was less than they had imagined it would be.

Secondly, even when a class was engaged in reading and writing activities, there were frequent interruptions by people from outside the classroom. Such interruptions might be caused by children bringing messages from other teachers, by the headteacher coming to discuss something, or perhaps by a parent wanting to see the teacher. On each occasion the teacher had to stop and deal with the situation – and frequently the children stopped too. Thus, the period which the teacher might think of as thirty minutes or one hour devoted to reading and writing could be whittled away, possibly by a quarter or a third.

The third kind of interruption to the teaching-and-learning time came from the children themselves. It is inevitable that a proportion of both teachers' and children's time in primary schools is spent on extraneous activities relating to organization, equipment, discipline and so on. Examples of such activities were children losing pencils, rubbers or books, water or paint being spilt or a child feeling ill. All these activities further reduced the time which was actually devoted to the task in hand.

Teachers' time
One of the most striking features of the schedule data was the number of times a teacher switched attention from one child or group to another during a twenty-minute period. This was parti-

cularly noticeable in periods in which the teacher was listening to individual children reading orally to her, while the remainder of the class was engaged in other activities; and also during periods when a proportion or the whole of a class were writing and individual children approached the teacher for help with spellings. Indeed in some cases the teacher was engaged in both activities simultaneously; listening to one child reading aloud and, at the same time, writing a word in a child's spelling book.

The average number of attention switches for all teachers in a twenty-minute period was fifteen; individual teachers averaging between ten and twenty-five. The maximum number of attention switches recorded for an individual teacher in such a session was thirty-two.

A second and related feature of the data was the extremely short period of time spent by the teachers in listening to the oral reading of any one child. Concentration on a particular child was continuous for only about thirty seconds on average. Frequently this was the full time devoted to a single child. On other occasions contact with a child may have extended to two minutes, but there were many interruptions while the teacher provided other children with spellings, commented on other children's work, answered questions or issued reprimands. Furthermore, only rarely was it observed that a teacher asked either a direct or open-ended question of a child on the content of his oral reading.

A third noticeable feature of the teachers' data was the proportion of the time spent by the teacher in additional activities not directly connected with current teaching-learning activities.

From the teacher observation data, it was found that teachers spent on average 25 per cent of their time on such non-teaching activities. This result strongly supports the findings of Hilsum and Cane (1971), Garner and Bing (1973) and, in particular, Boydell (1974). The 75 per cent of their time in which teachers were directly involved in teaching-learning activities, was divided between the different categories on the observation schedules, in the proportions shown in Table 2.

Again these results support the findings of Boydell (1974), particularly in the low proportion (11 per cent) of teachers' time spent in higher level cognitive contributions (i.e. according to Boydell's definition, categories 3 and 8 in Table 2).

**Table 2   Proportions of all* teachers' observed time spent
in categories of teaching activities**

Category	Activity	Percentage of time
1	Gives direct reading instruction.	4
2	Recounts or reads from a book.	5
3	Explains or expands book content.	4
4	Organizes/supervises reading/writing activity.	13
5	Hears oral reading.	14
6	Supplies word/spelling.	6
7	Directs copying or literal recall.	6
8	Requires pupils' ideas on reading/ writing.	7
9	Comments on reading/writing.	11
10	Engaged in other teaching activities.	5

* The figures for first and second year teachers separately were remarkably similar.

Garner and Bing (1973) suggest that the very high incidence of teacher contact with individual children (illustrated by the high rate of attention switches found in the present study) may preclude any substantial work on a higher cognitive level than direct recall questions and factual statements.

Children's time

Bearing in mind that the children observed were a random sample from the band of children of average reading attainment in each class, teachers may be surprised at certain of the patterns of activities shown up by the records of children's observation schedules.

1   Time spent non-orientated

The first noteworthy feature of the children's data was the amount of time spent by many children in what are termed non-orientated activities. These are activities which are not clearly directed towards the activity in hand. They include talking to other children, searching for pencils, wandering about the room or waiting to gain the teacher's attention. (The latter activity was differentiated from the other non-orientated activities on the record sheet.)

Of course, it would be unrealistic to expect children of seven and eight years old always to concentrate totally on the task in hand. Indeed, most adults are unable to focus their entire attention on a mental task for long periods without being distracted for even a few seconds. Analysis of the 195 children's schedules in this research indicates that the average proportion of time spent on non-orientated activity was approximately one-third.

However, the proportion of approximately two-thirds of children's time being spent task-orientated and one-third non-orientated presents too optimistic a picture of what actually happened over a longer period. When observation sessions occasionally extended to a complete hour with the same class, it was noted that the proportion of children's time spent on non-orientated activities over the whole period was much greater. As every teacher knows, it often takes the first five or ten minutes of a period for all children to become task-orientated. Then, after an initial period of reasonably high concentration for most children, as the hour progresses task-orientation decreases and non-orientation increases. Many of the twenty-minute observation periods recorded in this research, as they commenced five to ten minutes after the children had come into the room and actually started work, might be described as 'heavily saturated' with reading/writing activities.

2 Children vary in their work patterns
The second fact emerging from an examination of the children's observation schedules was that, not only did children exhibit differences in their average levels of task-orientation, but their own degrees of concentration varied from one period to another. Quite often the reasons for variations in an individual child's task-orientation could be traced to motivation. The example of one first-year boy on five different occasions illustrates this point.

This boy's average task-orientation over seven observed periods was 62·5 per cent. In the first three periods the concentration he demonstrated was far above average. When background knowledge of this boy and of the lessons observed are related to the observation records, it becomes apparent that motivation and interest can dramatically alter the ratio of task-orientated to non-orientated activities. In the first example (concentration 90 per cent), he was reading from his own *Wide Range Reader*. In the third example (concentration 80 per cent), he was writing about a self-selected book he had read. In the fourth example (concentration 70 per cent), every child in the class had been asked to write a story which he or she had composed. In the final example, when the boy's task-orientated activities had dropped well below average (32 per cent), the children were doing free writing about Eskimos, following a television programme. This particular pattern of an increase in non-orientation in free writing periods was one frequently noted in the observation records.

3 Task-orientation can be unproductive
One further point to mention here is that children can sometimes appear to be highly task-orientated without this proving fruitful. An example which illustrates this is that of a first-year girl (Sheila) who, during one observation period, spent 55 per cent of her time task-orientated. The task set by the teacher was for her to copy certain small pictures from her reading book (*Oxford Colour Reader*) and then write something under each one. However, although the child worked fairly diligently on what her teacher had asked her to do, her reading and writing activities were minimal. Of the twenty-two recorded task-orientated activities, eighteen involved merely drawing. Only four of the recordings (i.e. two minutes) related to reading and writing activities and so were in any way likely to contribute to her reading progress.

Teachers' time compared with children's time
The optimum use of teachers' and children's time would seem to be desirable objectives. Accordingly, the intensity with which teachers work in most reading and writing sessions needs to be examined alongside the corresponding patterns of activities of the children in their classes. With regard to the girl, Sheila, previously referred to, it is worth examining what her teacher was doing during this reading period. All the children were engaged in activities such as reading, writing, answering questions or drawing, connected with their basic reading books – *Wide Range*

Readers and/or the related *Quiz Books* or *Oxford Colour Readers*. The teacher was sitting at her table and calling out individual children to read to her. Other children continued to ask the teacher's help with spellings or other queries. In other words, it was the kind of period which forms a regular feature of the majority of first-year junior classes.

From a breakdown of one teacher's activities it can be seen that in a twenty-minute period, the teacher had contact with eighteen children. In nine cases she was listening to the child reading, while nine other children came to show written work or ask for help. Most of the contacts with individual children were of thirty seconds or less. The longest contact was of two and a half minutes – with one interruption. While the teacher was working at this terrific pace, the girl, Sheila, was reading or writing only four out of the forty recording times.

Summary
The following points represent a summary of tentative findings based on a preliminary examination of one aspect of the observation schedules, which were devised and used in the project.

1　Less time was spent on reading and writing activities than teachers might have imagined. The reduction in the anticipated time can be attributed to:
　(a)　alterations to the normal routine of class or school
　(b)　interruptions to lessons caused by other people entering the classroom
　(c)　interruptions caused by children in the class.
2　In many reading and writing periods teachers worked extremely hard, continually switching their attention from one child or group to another.
3　One result of this was that the time devoted to listening to any one child reading aloud was minimal, frequently no more than thirty seconds for each.
4　Children demonstrated different overall patterns of work. Some showed up as usually task-orientated while others generally exhibited a low level of concentration.
5　Even so, the same child did, on different occasions, exhibit quite wide variations in the proportion of time he spent task-

orientated and non-orientated. These variations appeared to be linked with motivation.

6 First- and second-year juniors spent approximately one-third of the time in which they were observed on non-orientated activities. These average figures disguised wide individual variations ranging from o per cent (total concentration) to 88 per cent.

7 The high work output of teachers was not always mirrored by high task-orientation in their pupils. In fact, in certain lessons, particularly when the teacher was engaged in listening to individual children's oral reading or, in a writing lesson, helping them individually with spellings, there were indications that with certain children an adverse effect took over. High teacher output was then related to low pupil output.

Questions for teachers' consideration
These tentative findings from the observation schedules are likely to cause teachers to ask themselves certain questions about their own and children's use of time. The following questions could well be among those which teachers will want to consider and discuss with each other.

1 Is it desirable that the stream of constant interruptions, caused by other adults and children coming into classrooms, should be reduced? If so, how might this be effected?

2 We know that teachers have high objectives in relation to the reading and writing progress of their pupils and also that they work extremely conscientiously towards this end. But perhaps it would be helpful to think more about teachers' output of energy – which is great – in relation to the children's learning. The question is mainly one of organization of the teacher's time and the children's time. As the actual time spent on reading and writing tuition (i.e. teaching-learning activities) is limited, should teachers be experimenting with ways of ensuring that this precious commodity – their own time – will be most profitably spent, so that as much learning as possible takes place? Is it possible that, if the teacher were not driving herself so hard, for example helping thirty-two individual children in twenty minutes, she could experiment with

methods of organization which might result in a more profitable use of the children's time so that they learned more, practised more and used their developing skills more?

3 Consider the two types of lesson in which the teacher's output of energy frequently showed an obverse relationship with certain of the pupils' patterns of task-orientation: the oral reading lesson and the free writing lesson. The pattern of the typical oral reading session probably indicates that teachers have been persuaded by educationists, and perhaps by reading experts, into thinking that individual help is *always* best. If this is so, should teachers question whether individual tuition is always necessary or always the most profitable use of their time, particularly when the contacts are as short as thirty seconds? Are there never groups of children, or occasionally, a whole class, ready for the same piece of teaching or learning experience at the same time? If so, would ten to fifteen minutes spent with a group occasionally not be a more valuable use of teachers' time?

4 Regarding the typical free writing lesson, with queues of children wanting help with spellings, is there scope here for experimenting with trying to reduce the queues? Especially in first-year junior classes, children certainly do want a great deal of help with spellings. The teacher wants to encourage them to be courageous about using new and exciting words, and not just to play safe by using only the simple words they know how to spell. But is it realistic to think that one adult can give individual help in this way to thirty-five or forty young children at the same time, without there being a good deal of pupil-time wasted?

What might be done? First, could the number of children engaged in free writing at any one time be reduced by undertaking this activity less often? If so, only a proportion of the class would be writing, while the remainder were engaged in other fairly self-sufficient activities such as reading for pleasure or painting. Secondly, is it worth considering encouraging children to attempt to write all words on their own, with the help of dictionaries, word charts, card indexes, etc? Then, when a piece of work is finished, the child might read it aloud to the teacher, who would help him with his spellings.

Thirdly, perhaps one ought to ask if producing an imaginative piece of written work is not too difficult for certain of the children in first- and second-year junior classes? Some of them have difficulty in writing factual accounts, even when common spellings are written on the blackboard. Certain children appear to have less fertile imaginations than others. Could their imagination perhaps be encouraged by asking them to tell or record a story, instead of trying to record imaginative ideas through a most difficult medium, not yet mastered by them?

The three researchers concerned hope that these comments will not be regarded by teachers as criticism but rather that the results of their observations will encourage staff discussions which could result in experiments with alternative patterns of organization.

References

BOYDELL, D. (1974) Teacher-pupil contact in junior classrooms *British Journal of Educational Psychology* 44, 313–8

BOYDELL, D. (1975) Pupil behaviour in junior classrooms *British Journal of Educational Psychology* 45, 122–9

GARNER, N. and BING, M. (1973) Inequality of teacher-pupil contacts *British Journal of Educational Psychology* 43, 234–43

HILSUM, S. and CANE, B. S. (1971) *The Teacher's Day* NFER

RESNICK, L. B. (1972) Teacher behaviour in the informal classroom *Journal of Curriculum Studies* 4, 99–109

SIMON, A. and BOYER, E. G. (1970) *Mirrors for Behaviour II: An Anthology of Classroom Observation Instruments* Philadelphia: Research for Better Schools

SOUTHGATE, V. (1976) '*Extending Beginning Reading:* an outline of the research project' in A. Cashdan (Ed) *The Content of Reading* Ward Lock Educational

SOUTHGATE, V. and LEWIS, C. Y. (1973) How important is the infant reading scheme? *Reading* 7, 2, 4–13

11 Children's reading achievement in relation to their teachers' attributes

Joyce M. Morris

Introduction

Politics, philosophy and economics naturally affect developments in education and *ipso facto* reading as the 'first R'. Likewise, at any given period of time, reading is affected by significant developments *in* and, hence, the pre-eminence *of* the various academic disciplines which contribute to the accumulation of knowledge in its own broad field of interest.

Characteristics of the pre-Bullock period 1960–74

Thus, one might say that, in general, the fifteen years or so before publication of the Bullock Report (DES 1975) were characterized by a concern for equality of educational opportunity and, consequently, for compensatory education in areas of underprivilege, whilst, in particular, reading research and practice, in the context of language and literacy, tended to be strongly influenced by the disciplines of sociology, social psychology and sociolinguistics.

The literature of the pre-Bullock period 1960–74 abounds in instances of the natural consequences of these three social sciences concentrating on home and neighbourhood effects. Examples in Britain include the work of Bernstein (1971) and his followers on sociolinguistic codes, and the researches carried out for the Plowden Committee in the early 1960s which, according to Wiseman in his Preface to *The Roots of Reading* (Cane and Smithers 1971), show that 'home and neighbourhood effects far outweigh school effects on the attainment of primary school children'.

It is also interesting to note similar 'sociological' trends in publications from and about other countries during this period. For instance, there is the seminal work of Labov (1969) on the non-standard English of American black children. There are also the international studies of *Reading Comprehension Education in Fifteen Countries* (Thorndike 1973) which found 'very little evidence of the impact of the school or of specific school factors on the progress of students in reading', and which prompted Chall (1976) to state, in her Keynote Address at the Twentieth Annual Convention of IRA:

> Unfortunately, some people think the results justify doing little. No amount of work by the school, they say, can improve on what the child comes to school with.

Bullock heralds an era of positive thinking about school effects
Both Chall and Wiseman, when director of the National Foundation for Educational Research (NFER), tried like other leaders to counteract this pessimistic view of schooling. Nevertheless, the prevailing climate of professional opinion in the 1960s and early 1970s was such that, in effect, the Bullock Committee's focus on schools and, especially, on the prime importance of teachers in raising standards, virtually heralded an era of optimistic and positive thinking about the effects of education.

This thinking was apparently shared by all the Committee members in so far as there is only one note of dissent and one note of extension recorded in the Bullock Report, and neither conflict with the views embodied in the following statement which, in fact, is the starting point for the main substance of this paper:

> If there is one general summarizing conclusion we offer it is that there is nothing to equal in importance the quality and achievement of the individual teacher, to whom most of our suggestions are addressed. All our recommendations are designed to support and strengthen the teachers in the schools, for it is with them that improvements in standards of reading and language most assuredly lie. (p. 513)

Bearing in mind the prevailing climate of professional opinion prior to publication of the Bullock Report, it is pertinent to consider what prompted this conclusion, especially as it is now the basis of exhortations by the powers-that-be, including the present Prime Minister. In other words, what was the evidence available to the Committee which convinced members that raising standards of reading and language definitely depends on the knowledge, intuitions and skill of individual teachers rather than, for example, on much-needed social reform?

The evidence available to Bullock

The evidence on which the Bullock Committee was able to draw is explained in the Introduction to *A Language for Life* (DES 1975). In the space available below, it is summarized in list and note form, thereby highlighting certain aspects of significance for the ensuing discussion:

1 Two questionnaires completed respectively by a random sample of 1,415 primary and 392 secondary schools.

2 Written evidence provided at the Committee's request by sixty-six individuals and fifty-six organizations, plus oral evidence requested from a selected number of each group.

3 Written evidence submitted by several hundred individuals and organizations in response to the Chairman's public invitation.

4 Special visits of Committee members to 100 schools, twenty-one colleges of education and six reading or language centres. These provided opportunities to observe teaching methods and organization in operation, and to talk to a large number of teachers in their classrooms.

5 A short visit to North America by the Secretary and two Committee members to study developments in schools, colleges and universities.

6 Evidence received from Scotland, Canada and the United States.

7 Information and advice from H.M. Inspectorate.

8 Drafts and papers of various kinds from several of the eighteen Committee members of whom, at the time of the inquiry, sixteen were or had been teachers, six were involved in teacher-training and five had both undertaken and published relevant research.

As will be seen, the composition of the Committe was heavily weighted on the side of teaching. Hence, commonsense expectation would lead one to suppose that the teacher's role played a prominent part in deliberations during its fifty-four meetings, and probably made its one general summarizing conclusion almost inevitable. At the same time, one must concede that such a responsible Committee would have considered all the types of evidence from whatever source as objectively as possible, and an unbiased account of it is presented in the Report. This being so, detailed study of *A Language for Life* should provide sufficient information to ascertain which of the above-listed sources and types of evidence caused the Committee to give pre-eminence to the teacher variable. In particular, it should reveal how much of the evidence for this judgment was research-based.

Research evidence

What then does such a study reveal? In the first place, the Committee did not authorize any research specifically designed to reveal relationships between children's reading achievement and their teachers' attributes. It did authorize a comprehensive survey of primary and secondary school practice by means of the two questionnaires previously mentioned. But this did not and, by its very nature, could not provide research evidence about the teacher's role in raising standards. Likewise, no such evidence could accrue from the special visits of Committee members to educational establishments, inasmuch as observations and interviews were unstructured, and the collected data were not scientifically analysed in relation to language variables.

As for the other sources and types of evidence, we are informed that the Committee could draw upon 'an accumulation of experience, a wealth of research – both published and unpublished – and a very wide range of opinion'. In which case, a careful selection of references for the Report was inevitable if only for reasons of space but, presumably, none would have been omitted which strongly support the one general summarizing conclusion about the teacher's importance. If this is so, the dearth of such references suggests that the conclusion is largely based on the expert opinion of a majority of those providing evidence combined with that of the Committee itself. If not, perhaps the Committee felt little need to support its central thesis with 'hard' evidence from professionally-conducted research. Alternatively, and equally unlikely in view of the inquiry's scope and the research experience of five members, the Committee might have been unaware of some relevant research. Or could it be that, in fact, comparatively little relevant research had been conducted from which the Committee was able to draw support?

An affirmative answer to this question was given by Gray (1976) at the twelfth annual UKRA conference soon after publication of the Bullock Report. As research fellow at the Centre for Educational Sociology, University of Edinburgh, he not surprisingly drew attention to the fact that the Report's conclusion about the teacher's importance reflected 'something of a turning point in the ongoing debates about the teaching of reading'. He pointed out that, although a large number of studies of teacher effectiveness have been conducted, 'the number of relevant studies linking teachers and reading is small'. Then, on the basis of the evidence he had presented, he concluded that 'further developments of the knowledge, intuitions and skill of individual teachers, at least as these are currently defined, will lead to at best trivial improvements in measured reading standards or the reduction of reading failure'.

Independent re-analyses of NFER data
This pessimistic conclusion, flatly contradicting the Bullock Report's central thesis, was followed up by Gray (1977) in a more detailed article for *Educational Research* on the teacher's importance in the reading process. Its stated purpose is to examine 'some of the general implications of the relevant research', and re-analyse 'the only available British evidence on reading and primary education in Morris's *Standards and Progress in Reading*'.

Gray uses the term 'competence' for what in *Standards and Progress in Reading* (Morris 1966) is an overall assessment of teachers' attributes called the teacher's 'contribution'. His re-analysis is not concerned with the data showing a highly significant, *positive* relationship between the teacher variable and children's reading *standards* or attainment; in other words, with the finding that 'good readers tend to have better teachers than poor readers during the last three years of their junior course'. Instead, Gray focuses attention on the small but statistically significant *negative* correlation found between what he calls teacher 'competence' and reading *progress*, expressed as improvements in children's test scores over the three-year period. Taken at face value, this runs counter to commonsense expectation by suggesting that reading *progress* is greater when juniors are taught by poor teachers.

Obviously, Gray decided to re-analyse what is in fact a tiny proportion of the complex Kent data because he was curious about this seemingly absurd result, and could not tacitly accept the explanation offered that it was due to the limits imposed on the better readers by the test used. In other words, Sentence Reading Test 1 (S.R.1) has a low 'ceiling' or, more precisely, an insufficient number of difficult final items, thereby providing comparatively little scope for children who were already good readers at the second-year junior stage to demonstrate their progress in succeeding years.

It is clear that Gray was intent on re-analysis for he was not persuaded to accept this 'test ceiling' explanation by the small but *positive* correlation produced when data were analysed for only the below-average readers and their teachers, i.e. the children for whom the test allowed ample scope to demonstrate their progress. Apparently, he was also unmoved by the proffered explanation that, although more in accord with the earlier findings about reading *standards* and with commonsense expectation, this correlation was statistically non-significant mainly because 'by omitting the above-average readers the teachers with the higher assessments were also omitted'.

There is insufficient space for a more detailed discussion of Gray's conclusions from his re-analysis. But it should be pointed out that he is not correct in concluding that 'Morris was obviously unprepared for the evidence on progress'. On page 75 of my report, for example, an explanation is given of why, despite the known limitations of Sentence Reading Test 1 for assessing the reading progress of able juniors, it was decided not to alter it but to draw attention wherever necessary to these limitations for the better readers. It is also important to note that Gray's re-analyses were concerned with only one of several aspects of reading *progress* considered in the Kent inquiries, i.e. progress defined as differences in scores over a three-year period on only one of the reading tests administered and not, for instance, progress in functional or classroom terms. Furthermore, although he felt it necessary to probe deeper into this one aspect of the research and speculate about it, he apparently did not do likewise with regard to the close association found between good reading *standards* and good teachers. For example, there is no evidence that he reflected upon the possibility that, if the poor readers had been taught by the good teachers, their progress, even defined solely in terms of improved S.R.1 scores, would have been such as to produce a highly significant positive correlation between reading progress and the teacher variable.

Be that as it may, Gray proceeds from his somewhat tenuous conclusions to assert that, in the future, 'it may be as important to understand why "obviously good" teachers and teaching practices do not bring about the expected improvements in children's attainments as to invest our energies in continuing to foster them'. Admittedly, this assertion follows a note to the effect that his conclusions are in line with the general trend of findings from his recent, unpublished review of the available evidence. But it is far too sweeping, at least in the writer's view. Certainly, as Gray suggests, there is a need for critical examination of stereotypes of 'good' teaching and, in particular, whether they take account of how well children learn. For only then will estimates of teacher 'competence' improve on those used in the Kent inquiries which he says 'represent the most carefully conducted and considered of investigations'. At the same time, there is an even more urgent need for researchers to develop better instruments for assessing the many facets of reading ability and, thereby, provide the means to settle constantly recurring, burning issues about reading standards and progress.

Post-Bullock British research

The NFER recognized the need for better measuring instruments at the beginning of the Kent inquiries over twenty years ago, and proposals to develop a comprehensive battery of reading tests were put forward to the appropriate funding bodies. Unfortunately, in those days, reading was something of a 'Cinderella' subject and, in the absence of a financial 'good fairy', the project never really got off the ground. This is a great pity because it was directed towards providing diagnostic as well as attainment tests covering aspects of 'functional' literacy. As such, its execution would have rendered unnecessary many of the reservations about tests made by the Bullock Committee and perhaps even its first principal recommendation:

> A system of monitoring should be introduced which will employ new instruments to assess a wider range of attainments than has been attempted in the past, and allow new criteria to be established for the definition of literacy.

Reading achievement
Looking to the future instead of regretting lost opportunities in the past, it is important to note that work has started on implementing this first Bullock recommendation. It is funded jointly by the Department of Education and Science and the Welsh Education Office, and the NFER has been entrusted with a significant share in the monitoring programme that is being developed by the Department's Assessment of Performance Unit.

The first national survey of reading ability using the newly-developed materials and instruments is planned for 1979. It will assess the attainment of some 10,000 pupils aged eleven and fifteen, and follow-up surveys designed to monitor trends and developments in attainment standards over time will be carried out in succeeding years.

Relationships with teachers' attributes
So much for reading achievement, but what research into its relationships with teachers' attributes has been reported or is being carried out in the post-Bullock period to date? Apparently, the NFER is not conducting any and yet, with the Kent inquiries, it virtually pioneered British reading research involving estimates of teachers' attributes in the school setting. What is more, a fundamental interest in the teacher's role in reading achievement was characteristic of all concurrent and subsequent studies I conducted on the Foundation's behalf, including the last to be published, i.e. *The Roots of Reading* (Cane and Smithers 1971) which, incidentally, has also been subjected to some re-analysis by Gray (1975).

The *British Register of Reading Research* (Goodacre and Bentley

1977) records very few recently-reported or ongoing investigations which, judging from the abstracts, appear to be concerned with the teacher variable, and even these seem unlikely to produce findings about the teacher's contribution to children's reading standards and/or progress. Perhaps this is because research about teacher effectiveness is beset with problems which, for their solution, require more resources of time, money and trained personnel than are nowadays available. In turn, maybe this is why, whenever any research relating teachers and pupil achievement is published, it tends to hit the headlines.

This is certainly what happened when Bennett's report on *Teaching Styles and Pupil Progress* was published in January 1976. In fact, it created something of a furore largely because it challenged the educational orthodoxy that informal methods are more appropriate for primary school children. However, the study has some obvious limitations. For example, *pupil progress* (though not confined to reading) means the progress of a single age group over only the final year of primary schooling, and the assessment of *teaching styles* is based on what teachers professed to practise rather than on classroom observations.

From a researcher's standpoint, Bennett's report is an easy target for criticism, and Gray seems to have lost no time in aiming his analytical darts at it. For, in the same year, he and a collaborator (Gray and Satterly 1976) published a critique called *A Chapter of Errors* in which they suggest that the report is merely a treatise in which the conclusions are not supported by the evidence presented. Not surprisingly, Bennett was not slow to reply to the criticisms made by Gray and Satterly, and an article by him and a colleague (Bennett and Entwistle 1977) states at the outset:

> On examination it was found that many of these criticisms were based on misinterpretation due to their lack of knowledge and understanding of the measures, methodology and statistical techniques employed.

Whether justified or not, this is likely to wound the professional sensibilities of all concerned. However, researchers who work in the difficult and emotionally charged field of teacher effectiveness must be prepared for their reported studies to be severely criticized. Where possible, they should also continue more rigorously to seek answers to such important questions as, 'What is a *good* teacher of reading, for which kinds of pupils and in what circumstances?'

Implementing Bullock without more ado

Undoubtedly, professional research workers with experience at the chalk face are needed to provide the 'hard' evidence for policy-making in education and, in this context, for what should be covered in the training of teachers if they are to be equipped adequately to develop to the full the reading and language potential of their pupils. At present, we have not nearly enough published research of quality to be sure of all the essentials, although those of us who have spent years in systematic observation in schools certainly know where some of the priorities lie.

Without the confirmation of further research, the Bullock Committee is also certain about some priorities, and devotes six paragraphs specifically to discussing its number one priority, i.e. the importance of the teacher in reading achievement. Altogether, references are made to only two relevant research projects, one being that reported in *Standards and Progress in Reading*, and the other the Cooperative Reading Studies of the US Office of Education. No suggestions for needed research are given, and the rest of the evidence in these six paragraphs is expert opinion confirmed by the school visits of Committee members.

Understandably, the Bullock Committee did not want to delay the implementation of its recommendations by insisting that further research should be carried out into teacher effectiveness or, indeed, any other controversial issue in the reading field. This does not mean that it was sceptical about the value of research; on the contrary – as is made clear in a final section of the Bullock Report headed 'A Note on Research'. It simply means there is so much that can be done to improve the quality of teaching and learning that it makes good sense to 'implement Bullock without more ado'.

In consequence of this attitude, there are now available to teachers inservice courses on reading and language development of a more comprehensive nature than ever before, notably those of the Open University inasmuch as they are accessible on a wide scale. There are publications designed to implement Bullock in that they are directed towards helping teachers to devise a systematic policy in each school for the reading development of all pupils and/or an organized policy for language across the curriculum. What is more, some recently-published classroom materials for pupils are also designed to encourage teachers, whilst working with the materials, to increase their own knowledge of the English language and of linguistic processes.

Despite all this, progress in implementing Bullock on the whole tends to be slow, and even some of the principal recommendations are at present non-starters – such as the establishment of a national centre for language in education. The reasons are complex and naturally include the depressing effect of the economic situation. They also include the continuing influence of those who, as mentioned in the introduction, believe that schools have little impact on pupil achievement. Hence, they advocate social reforms which naturally have mass political appeal instead of supporting the Bullock Report's recommendations, all of which are designed 'to support and strengthen the teachers in the schools'.

What then can be done to convince the opposition of the importance of the teacher's contribution especially to children's reading achievement? The answer must be to build on what we already know about the teacher variable and provide more 'hard' evidence from research. In this respect, the United Kingdom Reading Association could carry on its good work of helping to implement Bullock as demonstrated by the entire theme of the 1977 conference. It could at least galvanize and stimulate further initiatives in this research area and, in doing so, back up more solidly the recommendation made in the Association's evidence to the Bullock Committee, i.e. 'the most positive step that could be taken towards the improvement of reading standards would be via the improvement of the understanding and expertise of teachers at all school levels'. In sum, herein lies the gist of a proposal to the Research Standing Sub-Committee of UKRA and, in effect, what amounts to a personal addition to the recommendations made to the Association by my Conference Working Party on Bullock Implementation.

References

BENNETT, N. (1976) *Teaching Styles and Pupil Progress* Open Books

BENNETT, N. and ENTWISTLE, N. (1977) Rite and wrong: a reply to 'A Chapter of Errors' *Educational Research* 19, 3, 217–22

BERNSTEIN, B. (1971) *Class, Codes and Control* Routledge and Kegan Paul

CANE, B. and SMITHERS, J. (1971) *The Roots of Reading* NFER

CHALL, J. S. (1976) *Reading and Development* Newark, Delaware: International Reading Association

DES (1975) *A Language for Life* (The Bullock Report) HMSO

GOODACRE, E. J. and BENTLEY, D. (1977) *British Register of Reading Research No. 2* Centre for the Teaching of Reading, University of Reading School of Education

GRAY, J. (1975) 'The Roots of Reading': a critical re-analysis *Research in Education* 14, 33–47

GRAY, J. (1976) ' "Good teaching" and reading progress: a critical review in A. Cashdan (Ed.) *The Content of Reading* Ward Lock Educational

GRAY, J. (1977) Teacher competence in reading tuition *Educationa Research* 19, 2, 113–21

GRAY, J. and SATTERLY, D. (1976) A Chapter of Errors: teaching styles and pupil progress in retrospect *Educational Research* 19, 1, 45–56

LABOV, W. (1969) 'The logic of nonstandard English'. Excerpts reprinted in *Language in Education* (1972) Open University Set Book

MORRIS, J. M. (1966) *Standards and Progress in Reading* NFER

THORNDIKE, R. L. (1973) *Reading Comprehension Education in Fifteen Countries* New York: J. Wiley

UKRA (1972) Evidence to the Bullock Committee of the United Kingdom Reading Association. Durham (mimeo)

12 Barking at Bullock–Reading screening: Barking's integrated approach

Muriel Buckley, Brian Daly and Geoff Trickey

In our view there is no advantage in mass testing and centrally stored data unless the outcome is individualized help directed precisely at the children who need it. (Bullock Report, chapter 26, para. 199)

The Bullock Report has inspired numerous screening schemes in local authorities. It is now clear that there is no very real difficulty in identifying literacy problems, their size and where they are most acute. There are, however, many potential pitfalls along the road to ensuring the desired outcome of 'individualized help directed precisely at the children who need it' – and not all of these are immediately obvious. The problems arise in making a day-to-day impact on the child in the classroom; in translating observations and test results into action.

In the London Borough of Barking an ongoing action research project was initiated by the Schools' Psychological Service in September 1975. Its purpose was to explore the possibilities of implementing an effective screening and intervention programme for first-year junior failing readers. Initially, collaboration was with just four schools. After two years' development the scheme has reached maturity in the 1977–8 academic year and has been adopted by over 80 per cent of the Borough's junior schools. A summary of the theoretical and practical insights obtained in the two years of fieldwork is described in this paper.

Our starting point was the search for what the Bullock Report calls '. . . a far more systematic procedure for the prevention and treatment of learning difficulties . . .', and so we devised a screening and remediation scheme based on the following six principles:

1 *Purposeful assessment*

All assessments should be as purposeful as possible; that is to say, where tests were used they would be tests with immediate and specific educational implications.

2 *Systematizing recommendations*

The writing of individual reports on children who have been diagnostically assessed is itself a very time-consuming exercise. One should perhaps exploit the advantages inherent in the fact that in the current state of knowledge our assessment expertise has its limits. There are a finite number of things that can be said at the moment about any failing reader. The principle of systematizing recommendations ought then to reflect this situation and allow explanations and recommendations concerning each assessable component of reading ability to be prepared so that they then can be brought together in whatever permutation the actual assessment of any individual indicates is necessary.

3 *Maximization of school resources*

This is little more than a recognition that to be effective the main impact must take place within the normal classroom. Few local authorities can employ sufficient remedial specialists to permit classroom teachers to offload responsibility for literacy problems onto them. It is the class teacher who has to be helped to deal with some of the organizational problems that arise in coping with those children in the class who have particular reading difficulties and this has somehow to be achieved without depriving the rest of the class of the attention to which they are entitled. We hoped for a fruitful cross-fertilization process between teachers, between schools and between services. There also seemed to be possibilities for making it easier to deploy available published material more appropriately by organizing it in relation to diagnosed needs.

4 *Devolution of specialist skills*

There was a clear need to devolve the skills of the Schools' Psychological Service specialist teachers. This principle is closely related to the Bullock Report's emphasis on in-service training. There was obviously no place for the sort of professionalism which might exclude the dissemination of the necessary knowledge and skill to the teachers in the classroom who are in the best position to use them. We are concerned here with making available a full range of identification, diagnostic and remedial teaching skills in order to facilitate and maximize the class teacher's contribution, rather than 'de-skilling' the teacher and undermining confidence by perpetuating the mystique of 'the reading specialist'. We are certainly not denying that there *is* a pool of expertise about the teaching of reading, but we are convinced that it could be made far more accessible.

5 *Collaborative involvement*
We wished to work collaboratively with schools in a spirit that accepts that there are no pat answers to these problems and that the teachers' knowledge of the classroom situation, of their children, of their school's organization, is vital to the preparation of any programme which ultimately is to work in that context.

6 *Practical back-up for recommendations*
Lastly, and perhaps most importantly, we felt that we had to do more than to identify problems and more than merely make recommendations. In recognition of the considerable and varied demands inherent in any classroom situation we saw the need to support recommendations in very concrete and practical ways: actually to give the class teacher an individualized teaching programme for each failing reader, together with apparatus and materials that would enable the child to be occupied usefully by the teacher even in the midst of all the other demands. Diagnosis in the absence of any possibility for remediation can provoke anxiety for the teacher and may actually be counter-productive. It was our view that specialist agencies like ours should have more to offer than a mere opinion in most cases, and perhaps the provision of 'expert' one-to-one or small-group tuition for a further tiny minority of failing readers.

The action research project
The implementation of the six principles gave rise to an involvement which was highly valued by the Schools' Psychological Service, by the schools and most importantly by the severely retarded readers themselves.

Identification

This proved to be the least problematic phase of the project. Class teachers collaborated willingly in carrying out group reading tests, scoring them and sending returns to us. There is an inevitable arbitrariness in defining the target 'at risk' group but we decided on a retardation of twenty-four months or more which seemed to give us workable numbers in most classes of between 10 per cent and 15 per cent of the children. However, in one class there were less than 5 per cent, and in another just over 50 per cent.

Diagnosis

Diagnosis is a very thorny area. None of us was satisfied with the published diagnostic tests available, some being too long and complex and many not producing information sufficiently relevant to the classroom teaching situation. We adapted some tests as yet unpublished and devised some of our own with a view to maximizing the educational relevance of the results. Certainty in this area of diagnosis cannot be obtained. Rather, what we have on offer to classroom teachers is a series of hypotheses worthy of testing out in the day-to-day teaching situation. There are eight essentially criterion-referenced tests for which we have collected some normative data. Three of the tests have been adapted from those described by Moseley (1975). The tests are divided into three sections:

1 Tests emphasizing *visual* skills
   (a) *Word retention:* a mini-learning test in which two words are taught 'by sight' and a measure of retention is obtained.
   (b) *Visual sequential memory (letters):* the test requirement is to reconstruct sequences of letters from memory.
   (c) *Visual discrimination:* discriminations involving attention to visual detail and two-dimensional orientation are required.
2 Tests emphasizing *auditory* skills
   (a) *Sound blending:* the child is required to repeat words which are presented split up into their phonic elements.
   (b) *Auditory sequential memory:* the test task is to repeat accurately lists of rhyming letter names.

(c) *Auditory discrimination:* a 'same/different' test in which words differ in initial, medial and final sounds.

3 Other tests

(a) *Concepts and vocabulary:* twenty items relating to the language of instruction of early reading constitute this test (e.g. letter, word, beginning, etc.).

(b) *Grapho-motor:* pencil-manipulation tasks relevant to handwriting are included in this test.

The tests can be used *selectively*, testing out a series of hypotheses regarding the nature of the reading failure. They are individual tests and take anything from twenty to fifty minutes to complete, depending on the child's performance and the tester's skill.

Experimental trials (using ninety-three first-year junior pupils, retarded by twenty-four months or more with regard to reading age) have shown each of the tests in the visual and auditory sections to correlate significantly with reading progress measured over eight months of the project. Not only is there accumulating evidence that the skills measured by this battery are associated with the early reading progress of retarded readers, but they are also relevant to educational decisions required of the teacher in teaching reading.

An attempt was also made to increase awareness of certain noncognitive aspects of reading in terms of learning and behaviour strategies displayed in the classroom. An experimental attitude/ motivation checklist was devised since there are obvious limitations to a purely cognitive approach to diagnosis. Teachers' ratings of each severely retarded reader were obtained along dimensions such as 'Interest in learning to read', 'Concentration', 'Level of activity' and 'Ability to accept help from others'.

In-service training

Two prime functions were served in in-service training over the two years. Firstly, it provided a platform for class teachers to give us direct feedback regarding the efficacy of our experimental teaching programmes and the practicability of the assessment procedures. Secondly, it was an occasion where class teachers could practise the testing skills required and participate in the interpretation of profiles. Profile analysis emphasized the teaching implications of an individual's skill strengths and pinpointed what appeared to be severe weaknesses needing attention. We worked from a position in the first year of the project where all interpretations of the diagnostic profiles were undertaken by the Schools' Psychological Service staff (see Trickey and Daly 1977) to the current position where class teachers complete their own diagnostic reports on their 'at risk' children.

Individualized programmes
The individualized remedial packs prepared for the use of the class teacher contained:

a suggested overall teaching strategy for the development of reading skills;
the identification of any serious area of weakness, together with a suitable strategy for its remediation;
details of suitable apparatus and schemes that the SPS specialist teachers felt appropriate for the child;
a detailed description of any deficit and its relationship to other functions important in reading, and its effect on the child's reading strategy;
general principles upon which remedial activities should be based;
specific suggestions for activities likely to help the child to overcome weaknesses and build on strengths;
a selection from a range of more than 700 worksheets, designed to help the class teacher in providing activities for groups and individuals.

These packs were collated largely from a stock of prepared explanatory sheets relating not only to each of the diagnostic areas, but also to a number of specific test profiles which have substantial teaching implications.

This growing range of explanatory, prescriptive and consumable worksheets is organized into a 'component programme system' now containing over 1,000 elements which can be selected and combined according to the assessed needs of the individual children.

Objective assessment

Follow-up testing in the original 1975–6 pilot study disclosed that the 'at risk' group of thirty-one children in the four schools had progressed by an average of twenty months in the eight-month duration of the project. These children had been working for only six months on their individual programmes.

The project was continued in 1976–7 when twelve schools were selected from the many that applied to take part. From eight of these schools, ninety-three children were deemed to be 'at risk' using the arbitrary criterion of twenty-four or more months' retardation according to the initial group reading test results. End-of-year testing – again eight months after the start of the project – showed these children to have progressed by an average of 23·5 months. A control group – of seven 'at risk' children in three schools not included in the intervention part of the project, but otherwise comparable – increased their reading age by an average of 10·7 months. The performance of the experimental group was nearly matched by a small group of 'at risk' children in a special full-time class of fifteen children working with a qualified remedial teacher. Here, the mean increase in reading age was 20·00 months over the same period.

Over two years there have been consistent and substantial gains in the reading ability of first-year junior 'at risk' readers involved in this identification and intervention exercise.

Discussion and conclusions

This project was an attempt to make a practical response to a practical problem. It was never considered as a purely academic exercise. The current theoretical debate about the acquisition of literacy skills is not all at a helpful level. There is a lot as yet unknown about the teaching of reading, but some consideration of the difficulties arising in implementing those principles about which we are reasonably confident, seemed appropriate. We hoped to get to grips with some of these problems, and to achieve some improvement in existing procedures.

Initially, it seemed that the Bullock Committee's ultimate objectives cannot be achieved without a massive investment of time. Yet on the one hand the class teachers already face a clamour of classroom demands, and on the other hand the specialist teachers face an impossible task if they are considered as the Borough's major 'task force' for literacy problems. The danger here is that in these circumstances the majority of children can easily fall between two stools.

The difficulties of the class teacher were clear. With perhaps thirty children in the class there can be little opportunity to give individual attention either to the elucidation of a failing child's problems or to their remediation. Indeed, one would be hard pressed to ensure even as little as five minutes with each child per day. This is the essential backcloth against which a screening and intervention project must be considered. There is then a need for realism and a willingness to face some fundamental organizational difficulties in order to avoid a morale-sapping discrepancy between a generally-recognized ideal and the sheer impossibility of its achievement for either the unaided classroom teacher or the hard-pressed remedial service. As far as screening is concerned, problems *do* need to be defined and their prevalence estimated, but there is a danger in this sort of exercise that the results may merely be the identification of a massive pool of need without any accompanying change in organization or allocation of resources to relieve the classroom teacher in the face of a publicly identified problem.

Our project package for identification, diagnosis and remediation was both complex and comprehensive and this makes it difficult to identify with any confidence which were the most effective aspects of the intervention. Feedback from the class teachers involved indicates that they particularly valued the practical nature of recommendations and the specific activities and individual worksheets supplied in the teaching programmes. It is our overwhelming impression that this material back-up, which facilitated the implementation of recommendations and implicitly recognized the plight of the classroom teacher, contributed enormously to the project's success. This involved a complete reappraisal of the role of our service and the reconsideration by class teachers of their own contribution. This basic willingness to forsake the protection of established roles and to try to cooperate and contribute 'according to one's talents' certainly resulted in useful new insights.

We cannot say yet whether the reading gains achieved to date will be maintained. Data concerning the Diagnostic Reading Test Battery is still being gathered and this is likely to require further development. We would also, in the future, like to look into the practicability of even earlier identification. Ultimately, one hopes that the components of screening – identification, diagnosis and remediation – will form an integral and ongoing feature of the education system, rather than this sort of 'once in an educational lifetime' event, but there is a long way to go yet.

References

DES (1975) *A Language for Life* (The Bullock Report) HMSO
MOSELEY, D. V. (1975) *Special Provision for Reading – When Will They Ever Learn* NFER
TRICKEY, G. E. F. and DALY, B. (1977) Diagnosing readers *Times Educational Supplement* 5 August, 17

13   The place of attitudes in the reading curriculum

James M. Ewing

At a time when curriculum development is a central feature of educational planning, the place of attitudes is now receiving some attention. Within the educational press and professional journals there appears to be a slowly-awakening interest in this confusing but important aspect of learning. For many years the interest in attitudes was restricted to only the most dedicated and painstaking of researches. For a long time the field of attitude assessment was viewed as a 'disaster area', and there will today still be many who share this view.

With the great expansion within the past decade of curriculum planning and curriculum development in reading as in other educational areas, considerable emphasis has been placed on the teaching of skills. The curriculum planners and developers have aroused a lot of interest in different ways of regarding the curriculum, different curriculum structures and different ways of teaching. Much more recently there has come about a renewed interest in the part played by attitudes. This is true of other educational areas as well as reading and is apparent in the thinking of educators from the highest government level to the classroom teacher.

The Bullock Report (DES 1975) opens with Part One entitled 'Attitudes and Standards' and then goes on to outline some of the attitudes to the teaching of English. Unfortunately little reference is made later, in this otherwise complete report, to attitudes to reading or indeed to the attitudes held by pupils. The subject is certainly not given the attention it deserves in this otherwise comprehensive text on reading and the teaching of reading.

The situation is a little better in the research field. The author is involved in a research project on the measurement and classification of attitudes to reading within a curricular structure. In the *British Register of Reading Research* (Goodacre 1976) there are at least six researches which are predominantly if not entirely in the area of attitudes to reading. In a comparable summary of mainly American research (Weintraub *et al.* 1977) there are at least twelve studies which claim to be looking at some aspect of attitudes within reading.

Similarly, in a whole range of Curriculum Papers published by HMSO for both the Department of Education and Science and the Scottish Education Department, there are listed for different school subjects, varying numbers of attitude objectives.

There does, therefore, appear to be a place in curriculum planning for attitudes, and, moreover, it may develop into one of the expanding areas of educational thinking and research.

What is meant by attitudes?
There would appear to be a variety of ways of interpreting the term 'attitudes'. The Bullock Report (DES 1975) refers to the views of those outside the school (e.g. employers) as well as the personal feelings of the teachers of English for their subject. The Report also notes the importance of pupil interest, reading for pleasure and the particular problems of those with emotional disorders.

When it comes to assessing attitude to reading Pumfrey (1976) mentions three British scales, none of which is commercially available. Little precise detail is given about exactly what is being measured but Pumfrey does raise the question about whether attitude to reading can be assessed as a unidimensional trait.

Perhaps one of the difficulties is that the word 'attitude' is not the correct word. It is certainly clear that when referring to attitudes many other terms are used, such as views, opinions, reactions, judgments, feelings, moods, etc. It would be helpful, therefore, to have a term which somehow reflects all these terms and yet is not restricting in itself. If 'attitudes' is to embrace all the personal involvements and the subjective biases as well as the reactions and opinions which are commonly interpreted under that heading, a term with a wider interpretation may be required.

Bloom *et al.* (1971) proposed the term 'affective' to cover this area. It would appear to have a sufficiently wide acceptance in educational circles for it to be used meaningfully in the present context. Attitudes to reading can therefore be interpreted as a wide range of affective components of reading; for example:

how good at reading the pupil considers himself to be;
the pupil's awareness of the purposes for reading;
how much enjoyment the pupil gets from reading;
how well the pupil relates to the teacher during instruction;
the pupil's willingness to approach a reading task.

These, and many other components, operate at different levels within the teaching of reading throughout the school and beyond.

There is no suggestion that the affective components of reading operate independently from the cognitive and skills components. Most would agree that, in every intellectual operation, even at a most basic level, there is an intertwining of the cognitive or thinking aspects with the affective components. Thus, as a part of every reading situation, there is some contribution from the individual's feelings, views, reactions, etc. The study of the teaching of reading must therefore have some regard for contributions from affective components.

A further difficulty, of course, lies in the assessment of attitudes. As mentioned above, the available British scales are somewhat restricted in their use. This difficulty is further compounded in the affective area when a relationship between affective components and attainment is demonstrated. It then often becomes hard to 'justify' a course of action. For example, if a pupil has specific weaknesses in the area of visual perception, then the work programme to overcome these difficulties has a fairly high 'face validity' – i.e. it immediately appears relevant to reading. If, however, a pupil has a poor self-image, not only is it more difficult to plan a remedial programme for this child, it is also much harder to justify it to the parents. The affective components of reading are perceived by parents and, perhaps, also by teachers to be less immediately relevant to reading itself.

Need for a general affective factor model
Many of the theories of reading are presented as models, even though the difference between a theory and a model is still dis-

puted. This is not the place to enter into the argument of whether a model is a theory that works, or whether it is no more than a graphical display of words.

With affective models of reading, therefore, the difficulties include:

the ill-definition of the terms and concepts;
the general diffuseness of the whole area;
the difficulty in observing and measuring affective components;

and these, among others, make it particularly hard for a theory of attitudes to be meaningfully integrated into a curriculum model. For example, the affective component of the interaction between the pupil and the teacher during learning is certainly important. It is very hard, however, to relate this interaction to curriculum planning. Several questions would arise, including: What is the interaction? How can it be described? Can the interaction be measured? How does it affect learning? Can anything be done to improve the interaction? etc. There will be many different answers to these questions – so many, perhaps, that the task of relating affective components to a curricular model becomes very difficult.

One important contribution in this area, made by Mathewson (1976) in the proposal of an Acceptance Model of reading, probably reflects the current trend of trying to identify the specific components of attitude. Although this approach is useful, it may omit the importance of something more general, more fundamental than specific factors.

The question may arise of whether attitude should be considered more in terms of a general factor or rather as a group of specific factors. If there is a general factor of attitude then it should be possible to describe much of our behaviour in these terms, in much the same way as 'g'-factor intelligence is used to describe the intellectual component of behaviour. A general affective factor model should be able to show a relationship between a person's general attitude and his behaviour. It may derive, thereafter, a number of more specific affective factors which are relative to specific behaviours.

The difficulty of assessing a general affective factor does not imply that such a model need immediately be discarded. It would at least require:

1 a very basic formula for each affective contribution to behaviour;
2 a structure to allow for the uniqueness of every individual's behaviour reaction pattern.

First, the formula to describe each affective contribution to behaviour. Possibly the simplest formula requires only two variables – the person and the situation. If related specifically to reading, these two variables would be the reader and the reading situation. Each of these two will be examined in turn for a general, underlying factor, in much the same way as specific intellectual behaviours are examined for 'g'-factor intelligence.

Factors related to the reader
There are many reader factors which can be identified, and the following is only a selection:

1 *Self-image* Each person has a number of self-images depending on the different roles and different types of situation. Each of these, however, can range from positive to negative in terms of effect upon behaviour. For example, the majority of poor readers consider themselves to be poor both in reading and in general school work. The self-image of these pupils is probably acting negatively upon their learning behaviour. There is a great deal of evidence to support this view, that a poor self-image is frequently associated with poor performance.
2 *Motivation* The degree to which an individual pupil is motivated or 'switched on' will itself depend on a number of other personal factors, for example the curiosity of the reader. If a pupil is keen to find out, this normally results in some degree of motivation. Therefore, books and reading packages which interest a child and appeal to his curiosity will normally be read. Similarly, the pupil whose curiosity is not aroused, who is not motivated, may find it difficult to become involved in a reading task. So motivation, like self-image, ranges from positive to negative in its effect on performance.

3 *Judgment of relevance* Pupils can be expected to make some judgment about how relevant and how meaningful they perceive a reading task to be at different levels. Such judgments may be made in relation to more advanced reading, possibly in terms of evaluating curriculum components. So some pupils can be expected to judge the worth and relevance of certain reading tasks or situations as they contribute to a broader pattern of work. Similarly there may be judgments about reading content, judgments which are close to literary appreciation tasks. The emotional component of such judgments may sometimes be forgotten in the planning of a curriculum.

In the earlier stages of a developmental reading programme, namely where reading instruction is still taking place, there can be judgments of a different nature. Many beginning readers see little point in coping with what is, to them, a difficult and confusing task. At their own level, these pupils make a judgment about the relevance of the reading task – and such judgments produce an emotional state against which the learning situation must be considered.

4 *Reaction to success or failure* The emotional involvement of the pupil during the course of reading must include his reactions to his own success or failure. This could be the success or failure in the process of 'mechanical reading' or 'decoding', or possibly to the understanding of the material. Most readers at some time become disheartened by a piece of reading which is difficult to comprehend. The pupil, therefore, particularly when he is still in the process of extending his reading skills, may be even more vulnerable to negative emotional reactions.

Similarly, the positive effect of success on future reading behaviour is well known to those teaching beginning-reading skills. The success of achievement is a highly-rewarding experience in its own right and normally leads to an overall positive attitude.

5 *Pupil awareness* This refers to how the pupil can identify what a reading task is and the ability to relate that to a likely reading situation. Some pupils consider reading in the classroom only to occur in very narrowly defined circumstances,

for example the class reader. Many other situations where reading is involved are not recognized by the pupil.

6 *Identification with the task* As with the other reader factors described, pupil identification with the task can function at a variety of different levels. The young child may derive considerable pleasure from reading because of his ability to identify himself with what is being read. Similarly, at a more advanced level, older children can 'take off' in their own imagination, through reading material wherein they feel an identity.

These are only a few of the reader factors, and each probably operates at a number of levels. They each have in common

  direct relevance to the reader as a person;
  a range of influence from positive to negative;
  some empirical support as correlates of reading performance.

Factors related to the reading situation
Again, the following is only a selection of factors:

1 *Teacher expectancy* The effect of teacher expectancy has been well demonstrated by studies such as that recorded in *Pygmalion in the Classroom* (Rosenthal and Jacobson 1968). In that study it was clearly demonstrated that children labelled as late developers did develop late, and those who were expected to make considerable achievement gains actually did so. In a similar way the teacher's expectations about a child's attitude can result in significant changes in pupil reactions.

   For example, there is likely to be a strong link between the teacher expecting a particular child to be poorly motivated and that same child's actual level of involvement. So the teacher who regards a child as one who 'just can't be bothered', may in fact be contributing to that very attitude in the child.

2 *Suitability of material* Every learning situation concerning reading will require some materials, even though at some levels they may be very rudimentary (e.g. flashcards). The suitability of the material can be considered with regard to

content; level of complexity; size; ratio of print to illustrations, etc. Few teachers would deny that unsuitable material makes a learning situation complex and difficult for the learner. The pupil's reaction to unsuitable material is a further complication. Material which is unsuitable makes the task of learning less structured, confusing and just plain difficult. There can be little justification for presenting to a pupil in a learning situation material which is genuinely at quite the wrong level of complexity, has the wrong content or, even, is in the wrong language. That is widely believed and generally accepted. But it is just as important to believe and accept that the emotional reactions to unsuitable material are equally vital. The child who copes is usually favoured with positive reactions. He has some feeling of success and he is rewarded by his teacher or by the system for being able to keep up with the work. But the child who does not cope with unsuitable material usually experiences negative feelings. He has some feelings of personal failure and frequently is out of favour with his teacher. Above all that he has the distinct fear or uneasiness of being identified *within his own group* as being unable to cope. The emotional overtones of the suitability of materials are, sadly, often neglected when considering a reading programme.

3 *The structure of the situation* Very often there is some security to be gained by the pupil from a structured, or even a disciplined, learning situation. Thus, younger children, particularly those for whom school learning presents difficulties, would probably find it easier to operate within a fairly structured set-up where the number of pupil choices is kept to a minimum. Such a child gains some security from knowing that his work and his responses are expected within rather narrowly-defined structures. This contrasts with the older, more competent child who can benefit to greater extent from the freedom of a less-structured learning situation, i.e. the child who, given the opportunity, can take the initiative and learn from it. In reading, the structure is often reflected in the reading material or reading scheme, the flexibility or rigidity with which it is used and the classroom system within which reading is taught.

4 *Competence of the teacher* This would cover a wide range of

aspects, some of them more directly related to reading. A teacher's competence in coping with classroom organization for reading instruction, for example, might be helpful for some pupils but not for others. There may also be situations where the older, more capable pupil has greater insight into an author's intention than does the teacher.

5 *Teacher awareness* As with most of the other factors, this can operate over a variety of situations and can range from the teacher's awareness of the process of reading to an insight into specific reading difficulties. The teacher's awareness may itself be related to the quality of teacher training and supervision, also to the extent to which a teacher is prepared to become involved in his classroom teaching.

6 *The tone of teacher–pupil interactions* By using the word 'tone', some type of 'emotional quality' is inferred. Teacher–pupil interaction within a learning situation can be analysed in several ways: source of contributions, teacher- or pupil-initiated, structured or open-ended, etc. Perhaps a more important dimension of the interaction is in terms of value to both the pupil and the teacher. Terms which could be used are 'emotional interaction' or 'emotional strength' and they serve to indicate that the tone of teacher–pupil interaction can perhaps be measured only in very personal terms and that it may even be difficult to express in words. An indication of this might be the personal satisfaction which the pupil and the teacher achieve from the interaction. It might also be reflected in the attitude which each holds about the other or the attitude each holds about reading. In whatever way the tone of the relationship is described, it is certainly central to the learning situation.

The situation factors listed above, like the reader factors, have several features in common:

a relevance to the situation in which a reader may find himself;
a range of influence from positive to negative;
some empirical evidence as correlates of reading performance.

The reader factors and the situation factors described are only a few of the many such factors which are possible. To satisfy the criteria laid down earlier for a general factor model, any combination of the above two sets of variables must allow for the uniqueness of every individual's experience-reaction pattern. In reality, each pupil's pattern of personal involvements and reactions is unique and individual, as is his range of experiences. This uniqueness is central to a general factor model and it may be achieved by placing the two variables in an orthogonal orientation (see Figure 1).

Figure 1   A general factor model

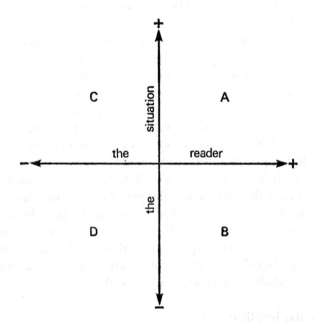

It is now no longer necessary to identify any specific reader factors nor any specific situation factors. The general concept of an underlying general affective factor should now be able to explain all observed behaviours.

Central to any interpretation of this model is the positive or negative direction of the factors present. Thus, a pupil in quadrant A would show the majority of his own personal factors (self-image, motivations, etc.) in a positive direction, i.e. he would consider himself at least an adequate reader, he would be interested and generally motivated to read, etc. He would also have most of the situational factors largely positive, i.e. the reading material would be suitable, his relationships with his teacher would be good, etc. Such a child would be expected to achieve well in reading.

A pupil in quadrant D would have most of the personal (reader) factors in a negative direction, perhaps through having experienced some failure or seeing little point to the reading he is required to do. He would also have most of the situational factors largely negative (for example, he might receive instruction along with the rest of the class when he really requires individual attention). This pupil might be expected to continue to fail as the negative conditions prevail.

The child in quadrant B has the personal or reader factors mainly positive, but the situational factors negative. This may arise where the child's reaction to reading is a good one, the desire to read is present and where he has good expectations, but where perhaps the material provided by the school, or even the teaching, is poor, uninspiring and perhaps not very relevant. Such a situation may in actual fact be quite a common one in our classrooms today, possibly more than we care to admit.

The pupil in quadrant C would experience the situational factors as mainly positive but the personal or reader factors as negative. Such a child might find himself surrounded by appropriate and stimulating material, have a good, interested teacher and have parents who encourage but don't push. Despite these conditions the child himself is still poorly motivated and unwilling, and probably, therefore, a failing reader.

Curricular implications

It would not be difficult to accept that quadrant A is the most positive in terms of predicting performance and that quadrant D is the least positive. Whether the order of priority between these two should be A–B–C–D or A–C–B–D may require experimental verification. Whichever order of priority does exist in reality, there are major implications for curriculum planning.

If the order of priority is A–B–C–D, then positive reader factors become more important than positive situation factors. The converse becomes true if the order of priority is A–C–B–D.

It is probably the second situation, in which situation factors are more important than reader factors, which most curriculum planners consider. Therefore curriculum development will focus on, among other things:

reading material appropriate for individual needs;
greater teacher awareness of reading purposes;
increased attention on learning situations to foster positive teacher–pupil interaction.

If, however, the correct order of priority puts the reader factors before the situation factors, then curriculum development faces a whole new challenge, with much wider focuses on:

encouragement of curiosity;
enlargement of self-image and self-identity;
opportunity for personal involvements and judgments.

Conclusion

The proposed model is based on the assumption that the affective contribution to learning can be explained in terms of a general underlying factor, i.e. positive affect produces effective learning and negative affect produces poor learning. The model also assumes that each individual's reactions to his experiences are unique and yet are comparable, on a broad scale, with those of others.

The major unresolved issue of this model is whether the 'reader factors' have a greater priority than the 'situation factors'. This requires experimental verification and clearly has implications for curriculum planning.

References

BLOOM, B. S., HASTINGS, J. T. and MADAUS, G. F. (1971) *Handbook on Formative and Summative Evaluation of Student Learning* McGraw-Hill
DES (1975) *A Language for Life* (The Bullock Report) HMSO
GOODACRE, E. J. (1976) *British Register of Reading Research* University of Reading
MATHEWSON, G. C. (1976, 2nd ed.) 'The function of attitude in the reading process' in H. Singer and R. Ruddell (Eds) *Theoretical Models and Processes of Reading* Newark: International Reading Association

PUMFREY, P. D. (1976) *Reading: Tests and Assessment Techniques* Hodder and Stoughton

ROSENTHAL, R. and JACOBSON, L. (1968) *Pygmalion in the Classroom: Teacher Expectation and Pupils' Intellectual Development* Holt, Rinehart and Winston

WEINTRAUB, S. *et al.* (1977) Summary of investigations relating to reading *Reading Research Quarterly* 12, 3, 233–565

14 On becoming a reader

Jessie F. Reid

How can more children be persuaded to read more books?
In her contribution to the collection of writings called *The Cool Web* the children's librarian Griselda Barton (1975) remarks that 'the more books there are published specifically for children, the less children seem to want to read them'. She goes on to seek a variety of explanations for this depressing paradox. She thinks, for instance, that adults can sometimes have mistaken stereotype views about which book a child 'should' choose to read. She also considers the possibility that the conditions under which children may be reasonably expected to settle to read for pleasure at all are becoming more and more difficult for them to find.

I want to look at this situation in the light of the main recommendations in the Bullock Report, and to suggest some answers to the question: 'How can more children be persuaded to read more books?'

In Chapter 5, the Report finds the roots of a love of reading in children's early experiences of listening to stories before they are able to read for themselves. This view is now so widely accepted that it hardly needs comment – except in one respect. The Bullock Report emphasizes – rightly – the social and emotional aspects of these experiences; but I think it rather neglects the linguistic ones. I am sure that the sound of words, the rhythm of poetry or good prose, the ways in which phrases are turned, have an enormous part to play in engendering a responsiveness to language. The effect was beautifully described a hundred years ago, by that great lover of language, Robert Louis Stevenson (1879). He recalls how, as a listener, he 'cherished the words themselves', even though he sometimes did not know what they meant, and how in his adulthood they continued to 'ring in his ears'.

The next point at which the Bullock Report considers the question of becoming 'a reader' – that is, someone who feels at home with books and turns to them for instruction and recreation – is in Chapters 8 and 9. Chapter 8 is concerned mainly with functional reading and Chapter 9 with literature.

Silent reading: its importance and its limitations

The first important thing to notice is that to be able to take advantage of written language at these levels of appreciation children have to be able to read silently. This is a topic on which I cannot find any discussion in the Bullock Report at all, nor is 'silent reading' listed in the index, though the mastery of it is patently assumed. Yet much thought has been given in recent years to the differences between listening to a story and reading it silently. At this point I should like to quote further from Stevenson's testimony:

> To pass from hearing literature to reading it is to take a great and dangerous step. With not a few, I think a large proportion of their pleasure then comes to an end, . . . they read thenceforward by the eye alone and hear never again the chime of fair words or the march of the stately period . . . But to all the step is dangerous, it involves coming of age; it is even a kind of second weaning. In the past all was at the choice of others; . . . In the future we are to approach the silent inexpressive type alone, like pioneers; . . .

There are here at least two distinct ideas of great importance. Nowadays, we are very accustomed to thinking of the development of the ability to read silently and fluently as a liberation – the casting aside of shackles. So in some ways it is: for there is no doubt that there can be a quality of absorption – of mental and emotional involvement with the import of the words – which does not come when the reader is reading aloud. But there is a school of thought which would take it as the mark of efficient reading to suppress all inner speech as well – or most of it – and 'read by the eye alone'; and it is an arresting notion that this could constitute not gain but great loss. For Stevenson, 'the chime of fair words' was something that might still be heard by the inner ear even when the lips had learned to stay still, and was an essential constituent in the enjoyment of a book.

I myself believe that we ought to be able to hear inwardly when we choose to and when the language warrants it – and this of course implies some ability on a reader's part to sense when it does. I think Stevenson is right in his view that this inner hearing can contribute to our pleasure; it certainly can give a stronger sense of being 'spoken to', it can enhance the reading of conversation, and in many cases language springs into dramatic life only when the words are imagined as being uttered.

The second point is that coming to read silently means a loss of guidance – one 'comes of age', becomes 'a pioneer' in the world of print. Now by contrast with its silence on silent reading, the Bullock Report asserts quite forcefully, in Sections 9.4, 9.5 and 9.6, the importance of thoughtful provision of appropriate literature in schools, the need to continue guiding the choice of books by pupils and keeping a record of their progress, and the necessity for the teacher to be well informed about what is available. But we have to read these recommendations in the light of Griselda Barton's despairing remark that the more there is available, the less children seem to read. Do they then simply need more guidance? Or is there, perhaps, something wrong with what our children are being offered to read on their own, or with the way we guide them into taking advantage of it, or both?

Good books for all children?
The rise of 'children's literature', now said by one writer in *The Cool Web* to be 'in its golden age' needs no describing here. But two years ago, at the UKRA Conference in Manchester, where the topic was 'The content of reading', some speakers on children's literature said some very surprising things. Of the two papers which I remember most vividly one was by Julia MacRae of Hamish Hamilton Children's Books (MacRae 1976), and the other by Nicholas Tucker, who is a psychologist and an experienced reviewer (Tucker 1976). Here, first, is a quotation from Julia MacRae, talking of how her view of the market had changed over some ten years: 'One part of me *must* accept that a good many of our publications will only reach the reading child, the committed child who already has sophisticated reading skills and can

appreciate subtlety of style and nuance of meaning.' And again: '. . . I recognize that we [i.e. her publishing firm] still reach only *the tip of the reading iceberg*' (italics mine). Nicholas Tucker, speaking on 'Books in schools – hopes and realities', remarked that, 'Many of the best books that are written for children are in fact written for a tiny minority, so all those slogans such as "A must for every nine year old" are often total nonsense.' These views were reinforced by other speakers at the conference. There is, then, an acknowledged mismatch between many children's books judged 'good' and the tastes and abilities of the majority of children, most of whom can – in some sense – read.

So what is wrong? Perhaps we could begin by asking how a children's writer who is not just turning out what Tucker called 'good rubbish' approaches his or her task.

One finds, on looking at what they say about their writing, that those who write the books that publishers – and reviewers – regard as children's books are sometimes curiously unwilling to allow that they write for children. Thus, Maurice Sendak (1975), answering the question: 'Whom do you see as your audience?' says: 'Well, I suppose primarily children, but not really. I certainly am not conscious of sitting down and writing a book for children. I think it would be fatal if one did.' And later in the same conversation he adds: 'I don't believe in people who consciously write for children.'

An author may obviously write for whom he pleases and one would certainly not want to disparage concern for the sources of a writer's creativity – sources that are often unconscious and ought to remain untrammelled. Also, of course, some writers – Sendak among them – do succeed in reaching many children even when they deny that they try to do so. But, judging from the evidence, what they achieve is not enough. We have to ask what more needs to be present as part of the conscious concern of a writer who will reach more than the 'tiny minority' – more than 'the tip of the reading iceberg'.

Writing 'at the level of the child'
Joan Aiken (1975) would say there must be a sense of involvement with the imagined children for whom the story is written. She believes that writing for children should be done 'purely for love'

and only 'with the whole heart' – a brave assertion, for she goes on to observe that writing for children is popularly regarded as a childish occupation, much less prestigious than writing for adults, and something you only do if you can't write anything else. Could this be why many people who obviously *do* write for children are reluctant to admit it, even perhaps to themselves, and talk of writing 'for themselves' or 'for the child that is in them'?

I want to put forward a view that not only opposes this rejection of a deliberate intent, not only endorses the view of writers like Joan Aiken, but goes further. I would like to make a plea to children's writers to write not only with the whole heart but with the whole mind as well. I think they should be informed about what ordinary children are like, what their limitations are, what kind of concepts and language they are capable of understanding, how well they can in fact *read*. Writers for children should be trying to *communicate* effectively with their child readers, and if you are trying to communicate with people it surely must help to know what they will understand. The limited appeal of many children's books – books which have, by more adult standards, a great deal of merit – lies, I believe, not so much in any deficiencies of plot as in the level at which they are written. Julia MacRae's remarks obviously imply a similar view – she talks of a child who can appreciate 'subtlety of style and nuance of meaning'; she talks on the other hand of those for whom reading is 'difficult, frustrating, unrewarding'.

I think, then, that we need a kind of children's literature which is, one might say, more disciplined. It need not lose the creative richness and the linguistic freshness that makes us call a piece of writing 'literature'. Indeed, much of the greatest writing we have in our heritage is simple and direct. There is no reason why these virtues cannot be used in writing which at the same time keeps its sights on those children who are just slowly building up a personal store of knowledge about the world, about imagery, about vocabulary and syntax. For every structure or idea not in the store has to be coped with – either deciphered or circumvented, either assimilated or set aside. I cannot see Chapter 9 of the Bullock Report becoming a reality if this rapprochement between authors and child readers does not happen.

Help the child to make the text speak to him

This brings me directly to my second question. I want to ask whether those of us who teach are doing all we might do to help the child to become a reader, to learn to approach what Stevenson called 'the silent inexpressive type' and make it speak to him. The Bullock Report has a good deal to say about how we can arrange to have, in school, reading experience that is to some extent corporate and shared, with the teacher ringing the changes between individual, group and class situations, discussing what the children are reading, letting them ask questions and so on. I like very much the section in the Report which suggests how this may be done. But I am worried about the placing of these key paragraphs. They appear at the end of Chapter 7, which is on 'The Early Stages' – and there is an implication that after the early stages such help is needed no more. I have become convinced on the contrary that this kind of reading experience should go on, for many children, for quite a long time in the junior school. I think that it should accompany the kinds of guidance, indicated in Chapter 9, to which I have already referred. What specific forms of help in becoming readers do the majority of children at this stage need?

First, they need to learn what Daiches (1948) calls 'cooperating' with the author – reading actively and not with 'sluggish acquiescence'. In order to manage this, they need help with the language of books – with the phraseology and idiom of storytelling, and the processing of sequences of conversation. They need to learn to sustain attention to what they read over a period of time so that they can discover the satisfaction of following the unfolding of a plot or the development of a character. And this means that what they read in the shared situation must include extended narrative and not just short extracts.

The recommendation in the Bullock Report that the provision of narrative material in the later years should be generous is in line with these views – provided that opportunities for shared reading experiences are there in the later years as well. Let me just stress, to avert possible misunderstanding, that children should, of course, also be encouraged to go off and pick their own books and get deeply and privately involved with them if they want – and are able – to do so.

There remains another obvious, indeed traditional, way of fostering reading skills – and that is through the use of writing about what is read. The Bullock Report devotes attention to this too, but mainly in Chapter 8, which is devoted to 'The Later Years'. The discussion is mostly about quite advanced work, involving a taxonomy of types of comprehension including critical evaluation, and other skills such as summarizing and paraphrasing. But long before these sophisticated activities are undertaken, what must children learn to do?

Interrogating the text

In Chapter 7, the authors of the Bullock Report recommend that children should become accustomed quite early to going back to the printed word and looking more carefully. This seems to me to be the foundation of comprehension activities of the more structured kind, but it involves an important new process, which one can call 'interrogating the text'. If we ask a child, in the context of reading a story, 'Why did Magnus crawl under the bushes?' he has to learn that if he can't remember clearly – and perhaps even if he thinks he can – he must go back to page x and locate the relevant part of the story and *find out*, or check on his memory from the same printed words which he read before. I don't think we sufficiently appreciate the magnitude of task-learning that lies concealed by the simplest exercise in 'literal comprehension'.

In the context of non-fiction, the need for the child to master this learning is clear. A great part of education is based on it. Can we equally justify its extension to comprehension exercises based on literature? There have to be some reservations. I think, for instance, that there are some kinds of fantasy on which you cannot set comprehension exercises. Also, the type of task set must be in itself simple, so that the purpose of it is not swallowed up in technicalities. I am doubtful, for example, about 'multiple choice' questions for young children.

There are, of course, some who feel it a kind of desecration to set any kind of structured task at all on fiction because such tasks involve 'analysis'. But if we substitute for this rather intimidating word the phrase 'seeing more clearly what the text could mean' then I think we can view comprehension work as one further aid to the development of a richer response to the printed word. I should like to end on a note of optimism. I think those of us who teach or do research are coming to see more and more clearly what becoming a reader involves. I am hopeful that the amount of well-written but accessible children's literature will increase. I look forward to a time when the 'silent inexpressive type' will speak to our children in tones so clear that they will be enthralled for life.

References

AIKEN, J. (1975) 'Purely for love' in M. Meek, A. Warlow and G. Barton (Eds) *The Cool Web* The Bodley Head

BARTON, G. (1975) 'Contexts for reading experience' in M. Meek, A. Warlow and G. Barton (Eds) *The Cool Web* The Bodley Head

DAICHES, D. (1948) *A Study of Literature* Cornell University and Oxford University Press

DES (1975) *A Language for Life* (The Bullock Report) HMSO

MACRAE, J. (1976) 'The publisher, the writer and the child' in A. Cashdan (Ed.) *The Content of Reading* Ward Lock Educational

SENDAK, M. (1975) 'Questions to an artist who is also an author' in M. Meek, A. Warlow and G. Barton (Eds) *The Cool Web* The Bodley Head

STEVENSON, R. L. (1879) Random Memories *Essays of Travel* Chatto and Windus

TUCKER, N. (1976) 'Books in schools – hopes and realities' in A. Cashdan (Ed.) *The Content of Reading* Ward Lock Educational

15 By adult standards: some considerations of the literary criticism of books for children

Margaret Spencer

Quality for the few – or for the many?

This paper is linked to the theme of the conference by Chapter 9 of the Bullock Report which deals with literature and the teacher's responsibility for the pupil's growth in reading as the development of literary discernment. The Report makes strong representation for the teacher to have 'an extensive knowledge of fiction appropriate for the various needs and levels of reading ability of his pupil', and insists that 'whatever else the pupil takes away from his experience of literature in school he should have learned to see it as a source of pleasure, as something that will continue to be part of his life'. 'Teacher influence and book provision' are said by the writers of the Report (DES 1975) 'to hold the key to an improvement in reading standards in the junior and secondary years', and they go on to suggest that the teacher's knowledge of what is available and her ability to promote it are crucial, especially for 'the less able pupil'.

The most recent information available to the Bullock Committee about the voluntary reading done by children in and out of school was provided by a Schools Council Report called *Children's Reading Interests* (Whitehead *et al.* 1974). In it the reading of children aged ten and over is considered inadequate in both kind and amount, and while many teachers do more than their fair share to promote a wide variety of books for children, many others are found wanting in their awareness of the range and scope of children's literature. Although the most important feature mentioned is the 'extraordinary diversity of book reading undertaken by the children in the sample', for the purposes of this discussion the interesting distinction made is between books written for children which are of 'quality' and those of 'non-quality'. The former are described as 'those in which the involvement of the writer with his subject matter and his audience has been such as to generate a texture of imaginative experience which rises above the merely routine and derivative'. Examples of quality children's narrative are *Alice in Wonderland* and *Paddington at Large*. The non-quality books are those 'whose production has been essentially a commercial operation, a matter of catering for a market' and include most of the writings of Enid Blyton. The authors of the Report admit that this kind of categorization brought into play an 'element of subjective judgment'.

Certainly one wants children to read and enjoy 'the best' of what has been written for them, but there is a developmental dimension in reading which is all too little explored. By making two crude bundles of children's books the Schools Council Report belittles the care and concern which editors, authors, critics and librarians have exercised as *their* subjective judgments for twenty years or more. It is scarcely surprising that the creators, producers and promoters of children's books set no great store by the discrimination shown by teachers. Left to themselves, teachers do not buy books which help children to develop in the role of readers. They are suspicious of narrative after the first two years in school. They buy books of information. Every year there are new storytellers of promise, yet their books and the ways by which they are judged are not of primary interest to those who could best use them. Informed awareness, if not actual textual scrutiny, of books for the young is not conspicuously a 'teacherly' activity. The Schools Council Report scarcely encourages further refined judgment. For all that reading and the teaching of reading exercise a whole Association, the teachers who flock to reading conferences are not conspicuous for their discriminating knowledge of what exists to be read.

As long ago as 1949 Geoffrey Trease argued that writers for children were artists in their own right (Trease 1949). His claim has been upheld by a group of critics who still dominate the scene of children's literature: Margery Fisher, Brian Alderson, Naomi Lewis, Edward Blishen, John Rowe Townsend and others, whose view that children's books must be judged 'by adult standards' has done much to support the editors in the dominant publishing houses. They have always spoken convincingly to teachers whose pupils move easily through the children's classics to adult literature and have steadfastly encouraged the extension of reading standards and choices, which had once been the privilege of a bookish élite, to children in general. But their criticism has its roots in an age with a view of childhood that no longer prevails. Their criteria are derived from books that are challenging to readers whose addiction to literature is assured. Many teachers see them as forming a charmed circle to promote books which critics admire and few children read. However, this judgment is a crude one and makes too little allowance for their sensibility and skill. In his book *Introducing Books to Children*, Aidan Chambers (1973) tries to redress the imbalance of 'inner ring' criticism of children's books by focusing first on the readers. But the idea that critics of children's books know nothing of reading problems is fairly widespread. The Bullock Report is not helpful in its failure to decide whether literacy now means extending to all the reading standards and materials that once belonged to the lettered élite, or a general raising of 'civic national' standards of reading that somehow include literature. The new and greatly enlarged audience for fiction is made up of those who are capable of reading all kinds of books and there now exist more kinds of children's books than traditional critical categories were developed to cope with. Discrimination and appreciation lag behind production. We are bound to ask all over again: what does 'by adult standards' now mean when applied to children's literature? Can we approach children's literature with Gertrude Stein's questions: 'What does literature do and how does it do it? And what ways does it use to do what it does?' and add 'For whom is all this done?' (Lodge 1977).

Extended critical writing, notably in *Signal, The Use of English* and *Children's Literature in Education* has always appealed to a small audience of teachers, along with special studies of individual authors and illustrators. The direct response of young readers to those who write for them, mediated by *Puffin Post*, for example, has enlightened adults. An increased historical awareness of the effect of readers on writers has proved fruitful, and the old formulae for 'adventure story', 'family story', 'historical novel' had been redefined by the authors as well as the publishers long before their rejection by Frank Whitehead and his colleagues. But it is the growth in the number of potential readers that makes new essays in criticism so necessary. If the 'best' books for children are defined exclusively so that only a few children can read them, what do the others read? Can critics of *children's* books ignore the developmental aspects of reading? What, for example, is a simple text? Is it the same as a simple message? What makes language readable? How does a reader 'take on' a writer's rhetoric and what view of the world does a reader derive from a particular author? What, exactly, is the nature of the code and the contact of a child's book? Is the 'adult standard' argument infallibly a good one? Do teachers want to be bothered with the criticism of books for children? There seems no end to pertinent questions.

Values and evaluation – in the child's terms

Teachers have made tentative steps to widen the charmed circle of children's books. The growth of reading matter for inexperienced adolescents is largely teacher-inspired – and critic-ignored. For all that much of it seems to me misconceived in content and unchallenging in style, a series like *Knockouts* moves into the gap between what some children learned to read before they were seven and others still need to read before they are sixteen. (*Knockouts* are paperbacks for less-experienced readers, edited by Josie Levine and published by Longman.) The selection of extracts, collections of short stories, especially when these focus on the nature of *literary* experience, are attempts to bring literature to the young in ways that speak to their condition. The *English Project* (formerly called the Penguin English Project, now published by Ward Lock Educational) with its thematic techniques tries to offer adolescents the means by which they can see themselves as readers in the adult sense, because their earlier experiences of reading failed to give them this opportunity. If the surveys show that the books which win most critical acclaim are those which fewest children read, then we have to look at the reading matter of those who might read the better books and don't. When English teachers read the Carnegie prizewinners they know that the problem for their pupils is not that they have difficulty in entering the world these novelists make, but that the language, the particularly literary forms of allusive speech, embedded references, subtleties of intonation and register, are unfamiliar. Children whose early reading experience is the book from the teaching series and the comic need critics who can sort out books that are good of their kind to meet these developmental needs.

In another vein, teachers have been foremost in the attacks on racism, sexism and other issues which deserve more than a passing mention. But here again it is possible to be sidetracked. Just as those who asked for 'greater realism' in children's books were rewarded by a crop of urban stories but no more significantly good ones, those who judge books by the author's approximation to a set of acceptable attitudes may find their didactic proclivities at odds with their literary judgment. Like Zola's *Germinal*, a book may teach about conditions in the mines, but as a novel this is only part of what it does. The 'felt life' of its characters, its making as a novel, cannot escape critical judgment. In this area criticism of books designed for the young is still at an unhelpful stage, and much wider discussion between teachers and writers about the issues of cultural diversity may make it clear that most adolescents' understanding of these topics is more advanced than their reading skill.

Where literature teaching has been at its most passionate and refined, in the tradition of Richards, Leavis and Inglis (reflected in the Schools Council Report), the contention that literature is concerned above all with values and standards has brought out again the insistence that teachers must re-examine what they are doing in order to make sure that their pupils are not given what is valueless. In a recent essay about *Watership Down* and the stories of Ursula LeGuin, Fred Inglis (1977) says:

We ask ourselves, as teachers and as parents, what do I want my son, daughter, pupil to have read, to have chosen to read, to enjoy reading out of the books there are? . . . If we challenge ourselves to say what is it for a book to work, then, allowing for our unpleasant and sanctimonious preference for being right-minded rather than purposeful and effective, we shall ask of a book that it make it more possible for its reader to face a brave new world which hath such people in it, to face it and face up to it *with a set of values* which are more absolute than expedient but capable of living with the facts of relativism and change.

It is difficult to deny this without seeming to sell the pass of what reading is all about. It is also difficult to move straight to *The Tombs of Atuan* from *Asterix the Gaul*. To build new critical awarenesses which teachers and critics can share, we must not simply engage in new demarcation disputes about which books are 'quality' and which 'non-quality'.

Two teaching approaches, fully adult, offer possibilities of a developmental study of reading responses in some depth. Aidan Warlow (1977) has shown that as the concerns of a reader change with age, it is possible to chart what comes into the foreground of his concerns. We all know that *Emma* read at fourteen is not the same experience as *Emma* read at twenty-four and fifty-four. We can demonstrate that a reader's response to a novel is, 'What happens next?' before he considers, 'Where am I in this story?', and that all readers need a wide experience of literary kinds and texts before the question, 'How does the author do it?' has any meaning, and that is still some time before the question, 'Is the author right?'. Some of my own recent work makes it clear that even quite young children are capable of *evaluative* responses, but the problem is to see these responses *in the child's terms*. The questions are best asked about books the children know well and *feel they have outgrown*. For an eight year old response may be to tell the story; a twelve year old discusses choice of actions by the protagonist. There is a time when a fourteen year old begins to discern the writer's path through a book, as opposed to the reader's, a discovery that often comes from something of lesser stature, like a detective story, before it is clear in *Jane Eyre*. Growth in response seems to involve a developing preoccupation with form, but not because it is the subject of English lessons. The best examples of this kind of literary criticism we have seen are books for six year olds made by eleven year olds.

The second stage that yields fruitful results to investigations of response is at the peak period of reading fairy tales and legends – about the age of ten. Elizabeth Cook and Bruno Bettelheim have given us clues by which we can interpret children's talk about them. Tony Aylwyn's researches (Aylwyn 1977) have shown how these stories are looked on by children as 'an accepted technique for discussing the chances of life'. Their notion of 'a story' is clear, but fluid. They are learning to look for an author but accept the fact that he is a little like God. They are still disturbed by first-person narrative. The fairy story offers them, in R. L. Gregory's terms, 'alternative views and courses of possible action' while the legend provides standards of judgment, concrete instances of fear, power, strength and devotion. Myth, however, because it is amoral and deals with unformulated laws of the universe, needs longer to become accommodated. It seems possible, from these studies, to show that children see 'fictions as the agents of change', a means of living one's life forwards. This is what Susanne Langer calls *virtual experience*, 'the illusion of life in the form of a virtual past' Langer (1953).

Children's fiction as a literary genre

Recent studies of the adult novel show that all the things which are actually present when children talk about what they have read, or had read to them, are part and parcel of contemporary criticism. Between the evaluative response of the ten year old and the studies of Iris Murdoch, Frank Kermode, Walter Benjamin, David Lodge and Malcolm Bradbury (Bradbury 1977) is a continuum which we could know more about if we looked at the ways in which children and adolescents *switch into* stories. 'Once upon a time' also means 'this is the kind of attention you give this tale'. 'Happily ever after' indicates the division of the story world and the one you inhabit; both are *real*. Recent books for children assume a great range of 'shifting' into the literary mode:

'A bottle of cold tea; bread and a half onion. That was Father's baggin.' (Garner 1976)

'In the misty morning of the world, when the Gods of Olympus still mingled freely with the sons and daughters of men, and Zeus, the King of the Gods, was dividing the fair land of Greece among those who were destined to become the ancestors of the Heroes who were to found its famous cities, there was a king in Argos called Inachus.' (Green 1977)

Each of these announces its intention: the reader's switching processes are distinctly different and the expectations likewise. Susanne Langer (1953) says of juvenile stories that they are

. . . skilful poetic creations – the whole fabric of illusory events takes its appearance and emotional value entirely from the way statements which actually compose the story are worded, the way the sentences flow, stop, repeat, stand alone, the concentrations and expansions of statement, the charged or denuded words. The ways of telling make the place, the action, the characters in fiction.

To chart the ways by which children become mature, competent and sensitive readers we must better understand the relationship of 'text' to 'message'. A simple-seeming text may have either a simple or a difficult message, depending on what the reader brings *to* the passage. There is a great deal still to be discovered about which books are 'easy' to read.

In a similar way we could reconstrue our theory of *genre*. At present this exists in two forms. First, as a publisher's categorization of 'kinds' – the adventure story, the historical novel, the 'time fantasy' and the like. Then as the total genre of 'children's fiction where the common elements are labelled as distinctive factors: child hero, ghost plot, happy ending, stable moral scene, lack of ambiguity in motive and action'. Dennis Butts (1977) suggests that this approach can be used to account for those authors who are equally at home in writing for adults and children, and for books like *Watership Down* which appear on both lists. Leon Garfield was rejected for the adult list and salvaged for the children's. Lucy Boston has never been glad to be considered a children's novelist. So, clearly, the way in which the author's view of himself and his art results in a book which is more acceptable to a child than an adult is still to be discussed.

The rhetoric of children's books is hardly studied at all, so that recent changes have gone almost unremarked. Where it was once essential to recognize the tropes of the primary rhetoric – 'once upon a time', the repeated refrain (I'll huff and I'll puff) which indicated the nature of the material being read, now the text may look like a TV script where the reader has to supply 'the visuals' on an inner screen of the imagination. The text is mostly dialogue down the middle of the page. Following Susanne Langer's idea of examining the composition we might look, for example, at how the text of a story for children *coheres* – how the choice of words which sets out the plot indicates the theme. The events are not only described for themselves but also for the underlying unifying principle of the story as a whole. As children discover the nature of literature they become aware – albeit unconsciously at first – that language is used in this way (Halliday and Hasan (1976)). Ordinary language used in predictable ways does not attract attention; used unpredictably it does. When Ted Hughes says the Iron Man's head is 'as big as a bedroom' he is both indicating size and domesticating his monster. There is also cohesion in form – the way by which incidents are related to each other. When the heroine of *The Magic Finger* turns her teacher into a cat, we are not surprised when, later, she transforms the neighbours. Studies of cohesion are specially relevant to writers like Mayne, Garner and Mary Norton in *The Borrowers*. As we study the texts in this way we could also investigate how the children operate the cohesion for understanding the story.

Towards a theory of children's literature
My recent experience of children who have failed to learn to read, alongside my work with those who have no difficulty, has influenced my approach to books for children in ways that demand of me a new definition of 'adult standards'. For example, reading experts suggest that literary language is harder to predict than 'non-literary' texts. The results of my present work run counter to this. If a plot is good, the unusual items of discourse are accepted without difficulty. Alan Garner's beautiful tale *The Stone Book* is full of such instances. 'Are you not frit', asks Mary's father as she sits astride the weathercock. The interweaving of dialectical forms is essential to the author's purpose and constitutes in itself a literary experience. The temptation to keep inexperienced readers away from these elements is to be resisted; they need language in all the ways that express the universal in the particular, to interpret another's experience in its link with language. The Opies show us that children do this for themselves. In looking at children's books we worry about the text and its difficulties, or about the message and its appropriateness. We need to look more closely at the fit of the one to the other by the standards now prevalent in 'adult' literary criticism (cf. Hawkes 1977 and Lodge 1977). If this could be done with more

sensitiveness, skill and knowledge, we might begin to bridge the gap between 'good books for children who read well' and 'other books for the rest till they can manage better'. My overriding conviction in all of this is that we cannot have theories of children's literature separate from theories of literacy. Literature is the driving force of learning to read: Margaret Clark's studies (1976) make that quite clear.

To bring critics of children's literature and teachers closer together we must ask them both to understand that children's literature is in a special and particular way about how the imagination works and how language transforms it into alternative worlds which readers inhabit so that the past and the future are both *potential* in the present. Children believe, as adults no longer can, that you can change the world by thinking about it (Piaget 1958). In a splendid essay about *The Borrowers* Nigel Hand (1977) shows how Mary Norton explores the possibilities of life by choosing characters smaller than humans but more powerful than children: the genuine *virtual experience* (cf. Inglis 1977).

Perhaps critics have been too self-indulgently enjoying children's books to give much attention to the changing conception of childhood that is reflected in the changing content of stories. For example, if you agree that sex and sexual relationships come into stories on the children's list, then the relationship between what happens in a children's book and in the outside world is actually changing. We need to look at the relationship of the 'real' world to the world of the children's story. It isn't what it was. We also might do well to look at the change of stance of the author to the reader. Who is the 'I' of the story in adolescent novels? Does the reader have to agree that the 'I' the author has cast for him/her is the one the reader is prepared to take on? Is the author still writing the kind of thing he (the author) would like to have read as a child? What would *The Rhetoric of Children's Fiction* look like? Aidan Chambers's essay on this topic shows where we might profitably go (Chambers 1977).

My thesis, therefore, is this. Literature asks the reader to read in a wide range of modes *and to recognize them*. At present the critics of children's books are too restricted in their recognition of the modes by which an author seeks to make a bond with the young reader whose vision of the world he thinks is important.

The critic, as the ideal reader, has to spot the change, to recognize new typologies of narrative and fable, to ask if it is true, as Fred Inglis says, that children's writers have 'gone inside' to avoid tackling outside issues. Literature depends on being read (or heard) as such, therefore a theory of children's literature is linked to a theory of reading and, because it is children's literature, to a theory of learning to read. In the same way, literature has to *be* there for this to happen. Children derive literary competence from their literature because the authors teach them the kind of reading their work requires. The importance of *story* is the belief that they share.

References

AYLWYN, A. (1977) M.A. dissertation. Institute of Education, University of London

BRADBURY, M. (Ed.) (1977) *The Novel Today* Fontana

BUTTS, D. (Ed.) (1977) *Good Writers for Young Readers* Hart-Davis

CHAMBERS, A. (1973) *Introducing Books to Children* Heinemann

CHAMBERS, A. (1977) The reader in the book *Signal* May

CLARK, M. (1976) *Young Fluent Readers* Heinemann

DES (1975) *A Language for Life* (The Bullock Report) HMSO

GARNER, A. (1976) *The Stone Book* Collins

GREEN, R. L. (1977) *The Tale of Thebes* Cambridge University Press

HALLIDAY, M. A. K. and HASAN, R. (1976) *Cohesion in English* Longman

HAND, N. (1977) in D. Butts (Ed.) *Good Writers for Young Readers* Hart-Davis

HAWKES, T. (1977) *Structuralism and Semiotics* Methuen

INGLIS, F. (1977) 'Spellbinding and anthropology: the work of Richard Adams and Ursula LeGuin' in D. Butts (Ed.) *Good Writers for Young Readers* Hart-Davis

LANGER, S. (1953) *Feeling and Form* Routledge and Kegan Paul

LODGE, D. (1977) in *The Modes of Modern Writing* Arnold

PIAGET, J. (1958) *The Growth of Logical Thinking from Childhood to Adolescence* Routledge and Kegan Paul

TREASE, G. (1949) *Tales out of School* Heinemann

WARLOW, A. (1977) 'What the reader has to do' in M. Meek, A. Warlow and G. Barton (Eds) *The Cool Web* The Bodley Head

WHITEHEAD, F., CAPEY, A. C. and MADDREN, W. (1974) Schools Council Working Paper No. 52 *Children's Reading Interests* Evans/Methuen Educational

16 Bridging the generation gap

Norman Hidden

The Bullock Report on poetry

Paragraphs 9.21–9.28 of the Bullock Report (DES 1975) deal with poetry. It is assumed that readers will be familiar with these paragraphs in which the Report recommends the reading of poetry as a form of 'shared exploration'. The Report goes on to admit that the treatment of poetry presents teachers with a difficult problem:

> The teacher is often faced with the task of showing that poetry is not some inaccessible form of utterance but that *it speaks directly to children*, as to anyone else and *has something to say which is relevant to their living here and now*. (9.22)

Nevertheless a survey of Yarlott and Harpin (1972–3) had shown how deadening teaching of poetry by exam-set authors might be. They found that 830 out of 1,000 O-level and A-level students in selective secondary schools in Nottingham declared themselves to have been put off poetry for life.

The difficulty is that the teacher needs to introduce the appropriate poem to his class at the appropriate moment, but in many cases he just hasn't the knowledge or the reserves to be able to do this.

As the Bullock Report points out:

> It is exceptionally difficult for the individual teacher to keep abreast of all the new poetry that is published. Indeed . . . there is often a time lag, so that the teacher is not aware of much of the work produced in the last two decades. (9.25)

Anthologies are not a substitute for the extensive reading of poetry by the teacher himself, for 'there is some very good poetry published that never finds its way into an anthology, and much of it would appeal directly to the pupils' (*ibid.*). The importance of contemporary poetry is that 'it has a voice to which a large number of young people can more readily respond. Moreover it is fresh to many teachers themselves and some feel able to read it to their pupils with the pleasure of a new discovery.' The Bullock Report concludes its section on poetry with a ringing affirmation that 'there are few more rewarding experiences in all English teaching than when teacher and pupil meet in the enjoyment of a poem'. (9.28)

These conclusions correspond with articles I had already written 'pre-Bullock', both in *Spoken English* and in the *Journal of the College of Preceptors*. I therefore propose in the remainder of this paper to restate my rather more detailed arguments for these conclusions. From the teacher's point of view the problem is one of bridging the generation gap. Most teachers are on their guard against the growth of the so-called 'generation gap'; they are aware that there is an inevitable age difference between themselves and their pupils. The awareness of an attitude difference creeps up more slowly.

As teachers of English our minds go back most naturally to our own early formative years and to those writers who seemed to us in or about our twenties to be the spokesmen for our age, or rather for our age group. As they grow older, we grow old with them. The generation gap has opened. And all factors seem to have a built-in interest in maintaining or even increasing it.

For instance, teachers coming to secondary schools from the universities, having read an Honours course in English, may well have finished at the end of the nineteenth century in their Eng. Lit. course. At school, O- and A-level set books are mostly drawn from the classics of the past. Again, there has been a welcome advance with some examining boards so as to take in well-established and middle-aged writers of the twentieth century; but these are exceptional. Inevitably, therefore, the spyglasses of literature are trained on the writers of the past. If a living poet appears among all this, he is invariably one who is no longer the voice of this generation, but at best the voice of the preceding generation.

Wanted: voices of the young generation

Scratch an English teacher with the question: What *contemporary* English poets do you read with your pupils? and the odds are that you will be told: Ted Hughes. Ted Hughes is still alive, and it is true that one definition of contemporary might mean 'still alive'. Rephrase the question, however, and ask 'What English poets do you read with your pupils who seem contemporary to them?' The teacher usually has no answer. His appreciation of literature has stopped a full generation before that of his pupils. Ted Hughes is a fine poet, but middle-aged; for him the genera- tion gap has already opened. In fact, all the best-known living English poets are middle-aged or older. Does that matter, the English teacher will exclaim. The children get tremendous pleasure, excitement, out of reading Ted Hughes (or Philip Larkin or Dylan Thomas or others). Yes, indeed they do, and out of Shakespeare, Milton, Pope, Wordsworth, Tennyson. But with each of these poets, the teacher has first to act as Virgil to his pupils' Dante and introduce them to a way of reading authors of the past that will make them become meaningful. He has to help them build the bridges which cross the generation gap. Anyone who has ever tried to obtain an appreciation of a great poet like Pope from children brought up on the Romantics will know the extent of the difficulty. The gap between our children today and the literature of the 1950s is not so great as that between them and the age of Pope; but even so, the attitude of mind of the fifties is not theirs – the assumptions have changed; the language itself has veered, however minutely; certain ideas and certain modes of expression no longer come so instinctively. Already, for the young, a conscious effort has to be made to put them- selves into the writer's brainbox.

It is probable (though of course arguable) that the most exciting poetry is being written by young men (and women) and that this has always been so. Milton had written *Comus, L'Allegro, Il Penseroso* when he was twenty-six; *Lycidas* had been in print a year by the time he was thirty. Pope had written his *Essay on Criticism* at twenty-three, *The Rape of the Lock* at twenty-four, and a great many other poems as well. Burns was feted as a national poet in Edinburgh when he was twenty-seven. Keats died aged twenty-six, Shelley aged twenty-nine; Byron had written nearly all of his poems by the time he was thirty, except *Don Juan*. Wordsworth had published *Lyrical Ballads* at twenty-eight; Coleridge wrote *Kubla Khan*, *The Ancient Mariner* and the first part of *Christabel* at twenty-five. Well, we know the Romantics flowered early, lived hectically, died young. What about the post-Romantics? Elderly, bearded, loaded-with-honours Lord Tennyson seems to contradict the thesis, until one remembers that the young Alfred had made his mark by the time he was twenty-three: *Poems* (1832) had included 'Oenone', 'The Dream of Fair Women', 'The Palace of Art', 'The Lotus Eaters', 'The Lady of Shalott', etc. Rossetti, Morris and Swinburne were all vigorous in their twenties. In our own century Wilfred Owen was dead at twenty-five, Dylan Thomas at thirty-nine. Even T. S. Eliot, 'the aged eagle', had published *Prufrock* in his twenty-ninth year and *The Waste Land* only five years later.

Of course, this is not to say that the work of these poets was not valuable after their first decade of adulthood. What one is saying rather is that their work as young men had that quality of articulating, in an exciting and authoritative way, the previously unarticulated, ill-defined, unthought-out ideas and feelings of their generation. It was this plus their technical skill which made them fizz. The technical skill continued throughout life in nearly all cases and may even have developed, but by then the generation gap had begun its inexorable rift.

To the best of his coevals even the most 'difficult' of new young poets, provided he is indeed the voice of his age, is never obscure; he is understood by them in a general sense even if not always in specific detail, almost intuitively. He needs no teacher to interpret him to his own generation, no explicator, except to readers of an *older* generation.

Where the sixth-formers find 'their' own contemporary poets, they will find a way of understanding them. Certainly the teacher has more to learn from them in this field than they from him. Few teachers have enough humility to accept this reversal of roles, nor do they take kindly to losing their role as explicators. They do not like poems which speak directly to the reader; they prefer complex and metaphysical poems and poems rich in allusions and poems which depend upon previous literature and poems which involve cerebration. In all these genres they have much to offer their pupils. That they might stand aside and let a simple, direct poem speak directly to the pupil, without explication, without comment, without analysis, is a harder thing for them by far.

Where have all young poets gone?

If the most exciting work of poets in the past was written before they were in their thirties, we need to ask ourselves where are the poets under thirty today? Why is our age an apparent exception to this rule? Baffled, we search around for names and mumble 'Brian Patten': the rest is silence. The cause of such paucity of published young poets lies not in their nonexistence – indeed there may well be more striking young poets about today than in times past – but in the depressed state of the book. Established publishers dread the sound of the word 'poetry'. As Anthony Blond put it in *The Publishing Game*, (1971), 'A publisher who set out to produce only contemporary poetry would not stay long in business.'

Hardback publishers waiting for the safe bet in poetry will wait for ever. Paperback publishers, like Penguin, have a little more scope. They launched the Liverpool Sound, poetry cashing in on the success of pop music. The rest of their efforts in the poetry field are far more modest than most people realize. For instance, their series *Penguin Modern Poets* is what in fact it declares itself to be, namely 'modern', not 'contemporary' poets. It began with Laurence Durrell (b. 1913), Elizabeth Jennings (b. 1926) and R. S. Thomas (b. 1913). These may be modern poets but they are not contemporary with our youngsters. The series continues with such poets as George Barker (b. 1913), Martin Bell (b. 1918), Charles Causley (b. 1917) - all good poets and deservedly in paperback, but they are not and cannot be (and would not claim to be, nor would Penguin claim them to be) spokesmen for the generation of today. The work of brilliant young poets is not appearing, for the most part, where it can be seen by the public or noticed by the critics, obsessed as they are with established publishers. It is appearing instead in the traditional spawning ground of new poetry, the little magazines and the little presses. Here are the new poets who might appeal directly to sixth-form pupils and college students, giving them a base of interest in poetry as something relevant to their own lives and times, and this interest is the springboard, as every English teacher surely realizes, for further exploration into the literature of other days and other times.

The conclusion one draws from this is that schools and colleges should start pretty smartly to take an interest in these little presses and little magazines, whose representatives do not call on their schools, who cannot afford to mail their advertising literature through the post, who are mostly ignored by critics and reviewers, and about whom there is very little information easily accessible. For these presses the educational market would be a godsend: if teachers would order their books and magazines for the school library with courage, if they would use the little magazines in bulk for classroom work, both as part of poetry appreciation and as a stimulus for creative writing, the financial position of these publications which handicaps them to the point of anonymity would be strengthened sufficiently for them to begin to operate in the open much more effectively. This would be good for the poets involved, good for school and college, good for poetry as a whole. I should emphasize that the little magazines in particular which could make such an effective contribution to sixth-form literary studies are those which place special emphasis on poetry itself rather than on reviews or critical articles about poetry: read poetry, *not* read about poetry should be the motto here. Magazines which come to mind include *Poetry Review*, *New Poetry* (*Workshop Press*), *Agenda*, *Stand*, *Outposts*. There are many more, some too ephemeral to be listed but good fun while they last, others too traditional to be really valuable, and others which I have probably overlooked or not mentioned because they contain too high a proportion of critical material to creative work of value. (This would exclude a journal such as *The Review*, for instance, useful though this might be in a school library in some other respects.) A full list is available in the *Poets' Yearbook*. Schools should not, of course, overlook little magazines published in their own localities.

The magazines named above are not expensive. School funds and department allocations are not to be spent lightly; but surely much of the neglect of contemporary little magazines is a matter of ignorance, and sometimes literary snobbery, rather than finance. Their value is in providing an immediate ground for discussion between the alert teacher and his pupils who pick up the signals of poetry on a different and more contemporary wavelength. And if the idea of being ahead of the herd appeals, this quotation from an article in the *Times Literary Supplement* of 12 February 1970 may be useful: '80 per cent of our most important post-1912 critics, novelists, poets and storytellers first published in little mags'. It is equally likely that 80 per cent of posterity's post-1972 writers are there too, waiting for the trained academic eye to pick them out!

References

BLOND, A. (1971) *The Publishing Game* Jonathan Cape
YARLOTT, G. and HARPIN, W. S. (1972–3) *One thousand responses to English literature Educational Research* 13, I, II

Part 4

Looking ahead

17 Recommendations for the implementation of the Bullock Report

Introduction

The 1977 UKRA Conference comprised, in addition to the usual lecture sessions, a series of sessions where Conference delegates formed a dozen working parties which had the brief of discussing how various agencies can contribute more to the task of implementing the recommendations of the Bullock Report.

Each working party addressed itself to one of the following five agencies:

1 heads of schools and teachers
2 Local Education Authorities (LEAs)
3 publishers
4 researchers and research bodies
5 the United Kingdom Reading Association (UKRA).

The task of the working parties was to formulate recommendations to these agencies concerning ways in which they might help teachers in their effort to develop and implement policies for language and reading. The proposals put forward by the Bullock Committee formed the basis for these sessions, as, indeed, for the whole Conference.

We are very grateful to the following prominent members of the Association, each of whom undertook to chair one working party during all its sessions:

Asher Cashdan, Sheffield Polytechnic
John Chapman, The Open University
Peter Davies, National Foundation for Educational Research
Keith Gardner, University of Nottingham

Bruce Gillham, Newcastle Polytechnic
Alastair Hendry, Craigie College of Education
Ian MacAskill, HMI (Scotland)
Joyce Morris, Language Arts Consultant, London
Donald Moyle, Edge Hill College of Education
Ed Ramsay, Remedial Advisory Service, Teesside
Derek Thackray, St Pauls College of Education.

We are also grateful to all those Conference delegates who took part in the working-party discussions and helped to formulate the recommendations below.

RECOMMENDATIONS TO HEADS OF SCHOOLS AND TEACHERS: GROUP 1

The group recognizes the constraints of money, personality, politics, tiredness and time. It also recognizes that not all suggestions will apply to all teachers and headteachers, and that there are differences between the primary and the secondary sectors. That being said, the group wants to make the following recommendations and suggestions.

Regarding the role of the headteacher

1 *Organizational style*
    The headteacher should:
    (a) provide a climate favourable for staff initiative and development
    (b) encourage attitudinal change
    (c) provide leadership where appropriate
    (d) outline policy guidelines but allow professional freedom to the teachers in their implementation of ideas.

2 *Initiation of training*
    The headteacher should arrange (in response to staff demands) various forms of in-service training, all of which should be school based. The following examples of appropriate forms were given by the group:

(a) people from outside agencies coming into the school to work with the teachers

(b) consultants assessing curriculum, organization, teaching methods, etc. of the school and feeding in recommendations

(c) teachers' self-training on the basis of analysis of teaching problems in their work.

The headteacher must find time for the in-service training programme. He can use occasional days, send children home early or free staff during school hours for discussion and action.

3 *Implementation of consensus*

Once staff recommendations are produced and agreed upon, the headteacher should be prepared to help in implementing them, by:

(a) altering the timetable

(b) changing his (the school's) priorities as regards the curriculum

(c) reallocating resources, i.e. money, staff, rooms, responsibility, etc.

The teacher's role

Regarding the teacher's role the group wants to make the following observations:

1 The teacher needs to be open-minded, and prepared to evaluate himself and his work systematically. Self-criticism leads to self-development.

2 The teacher needs to be 'teamwork-minded' and have a flexible attitude to teaching.

3 The teacher must actively participate in the planning of a policy for language across the curriculum.

4 The teacher should try to take advantage of opportunities for further training and in-service training.

5 The problem of the teacher's professional commitment in relation to his contractual obligations was recognized by the group, but it was agreed that this problem needs further discussion.

RECOMMENDATIONS TO HEADS OF SCHOOLS AND TEACHERS: GROUP 2

1 LEAS should be petitioned by Heads and teachers:
   (a) to define in terms of existing advanced reading courses, national as well as local, the 'suitably-qualified teacher' mentioned in the Bullock Report principal recommendation no. 4
   (b) to give priority for places on such courses to existing promoted staff
   (c) to extend an offer of places remaining thereafter to 'interested', non-promoted teachers.
2 In order to encourage the participation of *all* members of staff in a school-based in-service training programme, time must be set aside during the school year which will facilitate the discussion of language-teaching problems without the distraction entailed by constant responsibility for the safety of the pupils.
3 When LEAS ask headteachers to develop, formulate and submit language policies embracing the whole school, the headteachers must:
   (a) be given time to ensure full consultation and discussion with all members of staff; and
   (b) be assured of a response from the staff which will be analytical in terms of advice given and supportive in terms of resources offered.
4 LEAS should be encouraged by teaching staff:
   (a) in the existing staffing situation, to recommend the reduction of the numbers of pupils in infant classes; and
   (b) when improvement in staffing ratios is possible, this reduction must be a major consideration in arriving at a complement for a particular number of pupils.
5 Headteachers should be directly involved in the appointment of teachers, particularly in appointments to scaled posts.

The above recommendations were accepted unanimously by the working party.

RECOMMENDATIONS TO HEADS OF SCHOOLS AND TEACHERS: GROUP 3

The working party agreed on the following recommendations:

1   that there should be greater involvement of inspectors, advisers, teachers' centres, and college tutors at the local level, in order to help to increase these agencies' knowledge about schools, staffs and pupils, so that they can provide sustained support for the implementation of the Bullock Report proposals
2   that these agencies (as in (1) above) take every opportunity to disseminate promising ideas and practices amongst heads of schools and teachers
3   that a means be found of ensuring the coordination and co-operation of these agencies in their efforts to provide in-service training support for heads of schools and teachers
4   that heads of schools take responsibility for communication within their own schools and for maintaining close contacts with colleagues in other schools, especially neighbouring schools; this will assist teachers in getting to know the policies of their own schools more throughly, and will promote an interchange of ideas among large numbers of teachers working in schools at all levels of the educational system in a local area
5   that heads of schools should find ways of providing time during school hours for the meetings of staff in small working groups, and that this be done regularly and continuously
6   that it be recognized that *every* member of a school staff has a professional responsibility for seeing to it that the agreed policy is implemented; one person (not necessarily the head of English in a secondary school) should have the task of overseeing the policy implementation
7   that the initial and in-service training of *all* teachers be given a greater language-reading component
8   that places be found on the timetables of pupils of all ages for regular sessions to support pupils in reading for pleasure books of their own choice.

RECOMMENDATIONS TO LOCAL EDUCATION AUTHORITIES

The principal worries and concerns of the working party can be summarized in the following categories:

(a) time (for those organizing and those organized)
(b) fragmentation (of the professionals concerned, of the areas of work, of resources and commitment)
(c) money (lack of it).

The following recommendations were agreed:

1 that LEAs should regularly review the range of in-service training provision, from the more informal work within the individual school through to secondment of individual teachers to advanced courses. The aim should be to create a coordinated policy for the support and development of language teaching in the schools. One aspect of this policy should be activities aiming at the development and fostering of the self-respect and professional confidence of the individual teacher.

2 that all LEAs should take *particular* note of the recommendation in the Bullock Report regarding screening, *viz:* 'LEAs and schools should introduce early screening procedures to prevent cumulative language and reading failure and to guarantee individual diagnosis and treatment.'

3 that all LEAs should more effectively involve classroom teachers in their policy-making. They should ensure that positive encouragement is given to headteachers and senior management staff to involve all teachers in open debate and decision-making in matters of curriculum development, resource allocation, etc. This should ensure greater commitment and purpose on the part of the teachers.

4 that all LEAs should have adequate advisory provision to ensure the effective formulation, implementation and evaluation of LEA policy on 'Language in Education'

5 that all LEAs should coordinate the relevant agencies and resources (including medical and social agencies) related to

the child's language development. They must provide clear and concise information and guidance to headteachers on the availability of these agencies and resources, and they should monitor the use made of them in the schools.

RECOMMENDATIONS TO PUBLISHERS: GROUP 1

The group agreed upon the following recommendations:

1   It is suggested that as part of the International Year of the Child, 1979 should also be celebrated as Children's Book Year in the UK.
2   The practice of conducting field trials of new materials is to be encouraged. Greater rigour in evaluating and modifying materials would be welcomed, as would the reporting of details of such work.
3   (a)   Teachers' manuals pay insufficient attention to the limitations in teachers' time and technical knowledge, particularly in the case of introducing and testing materials. Many materials would be used more effectively if greater brevity and clarity could be observed in introducing and explaining them.
    (b)   It is particularly useful for teachers to meet and listen to the individuals who have devised or worked on the materials produced by publishers. The opportunity to employ this method of presenting materials should be taken as often as possible by publishers.
4   The agencies which exist to evaluate and disseminate published materials (e.g. teachers' centres, advisory panels, inspectors/advisers) perform an essential function. The publishers are encouraged to be more generous in supplying their materials to such agencies.
5   The group fears that the current interest in basic literacy will be interpreted by publishers as a need for re-issue of simplistic and 'mechanical' materials of a kind commonly used twenty years ago. The need is for the development and production of new approaches and materials – not for the resurrection of old ones.

6 To match the teachers' increasing awareness of the language demands of *all* subjects in the curriculum (technical terms, idiosyncrasies of language within discipline boundaries), consideration should be given to subject-based school publications which have the language demands of the subjects as their main focus.

RECOMMENDATIONS TO PUBLISHERS: GROUP 2

There was consensus in the group about the following suggestions:

1 Publishers should continue to improve the quality of reference books, considering in particular:
   (a) the presentation of the material/content
   (b) the developing of arguments rather than the presenting of facts
   (c) leading children into the effective use of a particular reference book or type of reference book.
2 Moves to reduce the teacher's opportunity to choose the materials to be used in the classroom should be opposed. Structure without prescription should be sought in this respect.
3 More materials are required for:
   (a) children of different ethnic origins
   (b) older retarded readers, for whom low readability level must be combined with appropriate content and interest level.
4 More attention should be paid to the role of illustrations in reading materials of various kinds and for various age groups.
5 A wider range of materials is needed at the secondary level – both in the field of fiction and in the field of non-fiction.

RECOMMENDATIONS TO RESEARCHERS AND RESEARCH BODIES: GROUP 1

Introduction
Teachers should be made aware of the distinctions between different forms of research, their purpose, methods and the particular relevance of their various outcomes. Three types of research were identified by the group:

1 *fundamental (professional) research*, not necessarily addressing itself to the application of its results nor seeking to provide prescriptions for the solution of practical problems
2 *applied research* which addresses itself to specific problems within areas of the school curriculum
3 *action research* where the teachers directly concerned are involved as 'partners' in the research work from the planning stage.

The most important way of achieving increased teacher awareness of these distinctions, and of how these forms of research interrelate, is by involving teachers in research (primarily action research).

The main practical recommendations
1 We need a great deal of research, both of the fundamental and of the applied type (see above), which is planned with regard to the needs and concerns of teachers and teaching.
2 Teachers need to become involved with research as active participants, rather than as instruments of the researchers.
3 Research results must be disseminated to teachers in forms which show in what way these outcomes are relevant to the concerns of the teachers.

Implications for the implementation of the recommendations
1 Initial and in-service training of teachers must focus on developing awareness and understanding of research and its relationship to practice, and of its significance and value to the practitioner.
2 Professional, or fundamental research (see above) has become

the stereotype in the minds of most teachers, but whilst the value of this kind of research is not doubted, research of other kinds needs to be promoted. Funding bodies need to be more responsive to proposals for alternative forms of research.

3 Dissemination of relevant research outcomes must become the responsibility of everyone working with teachers: course designers and lecturers in initial and in-service teacher training; teachers' centres; advisers and inspectors at local, regional and national levels.

4 Present forms of publication are rarely satisfactory for dissemination to teachers. Research reports must be written or rewritten so that they are more accessible to teachers.

5 The dissemination of research results needs to spread much more widely throughout the education profession, so that individuals who want to apply the results can be supported by colleagues.

6 The limitations of research results should be made clear to teachers. This is just as important as informing teachers about what the results are.

Areas for future research
The group considered the following as the most important areas of investigation:

1 what teachers need to know about language (including listening, talking, reading and writing)
2 the uses of language in the classroom
3 analysis of interactions in the classroom between teacher and pupils and among pupils
4 language and its relationship to learning
5 planning the language arts curriculum, recognizing the needs and requirements in 'life after school'.

RECOMMENDATIONS TO RESEARCHERS AND RESEARCH BODIES: GROUP 2

Introduction
There is no clear-cut distinction between teaching and research.

Research is, and always has been, part of the professional role of the teacher.

We define educational research as disciplined inquiry into problems identified by teachers and other educators. There are different kinds, which take different forms according to their different purposes, for example:

(a) *action research*, e.g. an investigation over a period of time into the effect of certain classroom factors on a group of children's motivation to read;

(b) *survey research*, e.g. a survey in a number of schools of the opportunities for pupils in a specific age range to develop their particular interests through reading;

(c) *formal research*, i.e. a form which attempts to examine the relationship between two or more conditions affecting learning opportunities and success.

Recommendations

1 The UKRA as a professional association should try to provide, through its expertise and other resources, encouragement and support for those working in *any* of the three kinds of research mentioned above. In order to do this the Association should develop effective means of communication, enabling discussion through conferences, publications and its network of local councils. Particular attention should be paid to improving existing, and developing new, means of communication.

2 During initial teacher training, students should consider the purposes of research, and be provided with the tools and knowledge to enable them to participate in small-scale investigations. Through such participation the students should come to appreciate the interrelationships among various forms and purposes of research. It is expected that the 'rigour' of research will transfer to classroom practice and its evaluation.

Similar approaches should be adopted in school-based in-service training courses, arising from the needs and active questioning of teachers.

RECOMMENDATIONS TO RESEARCHERS AND RESEARCH BODIES: GROUP 3

The group agreed to recommend that:

1 a means should be created for obtaining greater interchange of research information, particularly at the level of large-scale, continuous survey, across traditional discipline boundaries, e.g. medicine, psychology, sociology, education, and this interchange should be promoted by a central panel

2 researchers should consider such cooperation that would make available existing data of appropriate kinds, with a view to rationalizing programmes of research

3 there is a particular need for continuing study of pupils who achieve academic success under adverse conditions, with the aim of learning more about how various adverse conditions can be overcome

4 further research be carried out into the significance of various personality factors in teachers and in children, and into how teacher-personality factors and child-personality factors interact in the classroom situation

5 there should be a coordination of classroom action and classroom research, possibly in the form of a planned programme over a period of years, for the purpose of evaluating methods and materials in the teaching of reading

6 the plans for in-service training of teachers recommended by the Bullock Committee be implemented forthwith, with special attention being paid to the implementation of innovations.

RECOMMENDATIONS TO THE UNITED KINGDOM READING ASSOCIATION: GROUP 1

The group put forward the following recommendations:

1 that UKRA publications should increasingly endeavour to provide a forum for the discussion of problems involved in the

implementation of the Bullock Committee recommendations, with an emphasis on solutions to classroom problems

2   that the dissemination of research findings from other European countries should be promoted, e.g. through the planned Journal of Reading Research

3   that stronger links be forged, within the UK ,between the UKRA and other professional organizations, such as NATE (National Association for the Teaching of English), NARE (National Association for Remedial Education) and SLA (School Library Association)

4   that, at local branch level, members of the UKRA offer to facilitate continuity of teaching approach and 'language across the curriculum' by offering to lead joint discussions among primary schools and/or among departments in secondary schools. Guidelines for this kind of activity would probably be welcomed by members of local branches

5   that LEA advisers/inspectors who are members of the UKRA should attempt to encourage their colleagues to take more interest in matters of language and reading. Subject advisers might then help secondary specialist teachers to reconsider their responsibilities for teaching English in general and reading in particular

6   that stronger links and more exchange of information with other English-speaking countries be encouraged. An International Conference of Educators concerned with language and communication in English-speaking countries might be arranged by UNESCO, following an approach by the UKRA

7   that renewed efforts be made to recruit secondary teachers as members of the UKRA

8   that a round table discussion of the next IRA World Congress on Reading be devoted to the consideration of the Bullock Report and its recommendations.

RECOMMENDATIONS TO THE UNITED KINGDOM READING ASSOCIATION: GROUP 2

The group put forward the following recommendations:

1   *UKRA recruitment*
The UKRA should strenuously prosecute a policy of recruitment
of a larger number of teachers, students and academic staff in
colleges, polytechnics and universities. A membership of less
than 1 per cent of the British teaching force is too small to
make sufficient impact in terms of understanding and ideas.
Meetings held in a series of schools, rather than in one central
institution, give good opportunities for recruitment of new
members and for the exchange of ideas. It should be kept in
mind that personal contacts are more effective in recruiting
new members than printed publicity.

2   *In-service training*
In the field of in-service training of teachers, the UKRA should:
(a)   influence other bodies (e.g. local advisers, teachers' centres) to provide more and better courses and greater
opportunities for teachers to attend them
(b)   encourage increased in-depth study of specific areas
within the Association's local councils, by means of
work-study groups and school-based action research.
The Association should make a particular effort to involve
probationary teachers in this work.

3   *Initial training*
In the field of initial training of teachers, the UKRA should:
(a)   press for more time to be devoted to training in the
teaching of reading for *all* students, regardless of what
age range they are going to teach
(b)   give help in the design of more appropriate courses in the
field of language and reading
(c)   help to define minimum requirements for the content of
initial training courses as regards language and reading,
and put pressure on the appropriate agencies to implement these requirements.

4   *Standards of expertise*
The Association should try to reach agreements on minimum
standards in the form of training and experience requirements
for various kinds of specialists in the field of language and
reading in education.

5   *Parents*
The UKRA should:

(a) organize meetings to help parents to understand the language needs of their children and to suggest how parents might provide appropriate help in the language development process

(b) provide readily-accessible publications of a practical nature addressed at parents.

6 *Publishers*

The UKRA should seek to influence publishers in various ways with regard to the quality and appropriateness of publications for children. In particular, publishers should be encouraged to give as detailed information as possible on the readability levels of books and other materials, in order to assist teachers and, especially, parents in their choice of children's reading.

18   Reading: curriculum demands

Elizabeth Hunter-Grundin and Hans U. Grundin

The various papers in Parts 1–3 of this volume, and the lists of working-party recommendations in Part 4 all constitute a wealth of information and of viewpoints concerning language and reading in our schools. Any attempts to summarize and synthesize this whole wealth of knowledge and ideas would inevitably fail to do justice to each individual contribution. When we try to sum up what we see as the most important trends and to state some implications for the future, it is mainly because we feel the need to 'stop and think' – to assess the outcome of the Conference with regard to its main objective: to contribute to the development and implementation of better policies for language and reading in our schools.

After such an enterprise there is a need both to look back – to see 'where we are' – and to look forward – to see how we can move ahead from where we are. Any attempt to determine 'where we are' as regards a complex educational issue is fraught with difficulties, and will necessarily require some personal, subjective judgment. Trying to indicate a direction in which we can move ahead with reasonable hope of success is, of course, no less a matter of personal judgment. We want to emphasize, therefore, that the conclusions and suggestions put forward in this concluding chapter are those of the editors of this volume, but in formulating these conclusions and suggestions we have drawn heavily upon the knowledge and insight of all those who have contributed.

Where we are
The Bullock Committee concluded that no one method or philosophy 'holds the key to the process of learning to read', and they also expressed the view that 'too much attention has been given

to polarized opinions about approaches to the teaching of reading'. This is a recognition of the important principle that many roads can lead to the same goal, and it is a healthy reminder to those of us who believe that we have found the 'true way'. However, this call for pluralism of approaches must not make us forget that any attempt to teach a group of children to read – or to develop further their reading skills – constitutes *one* approach. The fact that several approaches are possible must not make us forget that each of us has a duty to develop or adopt in our work a reasonably consistent and comprehensive approach to reading and the teaching of reading.

Many of the contributions to this volume have something to say on the extremely important issue 'what approach?'. These contributions represent somewhat different positions, but they also have something in common, they place reading firmly in the context of language, of communication of meaning. This may at first seem rather trivial, since reading always is – and always has been – reading of language for a communication purpose. But the *teaching* of reading has not always recognized this fundamental principle. The teaching of reading has often been – and still is in many cases – narrowly conceived as concerned mainly with the translation of written language into spoken language, sometimes even more narrowly as a question of *pronouncing* the written language.

Narrowly conceived, reading can be seen as a mechanical activity which can be exactly performed in accordance with a set of strict rules. Teaching of reading is, thus conceived, mainly a technical problem of teaching those strict, well-defined rules. Probably none of the contributors to this volume would deny that there are fairly strict rules regarding how written language relates to spoken language. What they maintain – and what we think must be strongly emphasized – is that reading is so much *more* than a matter of these rules. They also seem to agree that the fact that reading is much more than 'decoding' or 'recoding' has very important implications for the teaching of reading.

The ability to read, in the sense of being able to communicate by means of the printed word, is an ability that develops in a stage-by-stage fashion. As soon as a child can 'get meaning from print' in a given situation, it makes sense to say that the child is 'reading'. It may even make sense to say that the child 'can read', but only if we realize that this ability can and must be further developed, at least throughout the years of schooling. No young child 'can read' in the sense that the teaching of reading is completed as far as he is concerned. *There are so many ways in which the ability to get meaning from print can be developed and expanded, and such development must be the objective of a long-term, continuous process of teaching reading.*

In the light of this view of reading and the teaching of reading, it seems reasonable to formulate a couple of basic principles, on which *any* approach to the teaching of reading should be based:

1   Reading is always a matter of getting meaning from print.
2   The ability to read is developed through reading.

One of the most important implications of the first of these principles is that children should, from the very beginning of their contact with the printed word, be made aware of this basic purpose of reading. This, in its turn, means that children's attempts at reading should always be attempts at 'getting meaning'. This is not to say that children should never be concerned with such things as relationships between letters and sounds. It is only to say that these relationships are of importance only as means to an end – as a help in the process of 'getting meaning'.

The second principle stated above, that children learn to read through reading, has also far-reaching implications both for the methods of teaching and for the choice of reading materials. This principle may seem like a paradox: children are supposed to learn how to do something through doing that something which they cannot yet do. This is, however, a paradox only if reading is conceived as a precisely-defined technical skill to be learned once and for all at the early stage of schooling. If reading is seen as a developmental process, where ability can be anything from the first rudimentary insight that there is meaning in print, to a very sophisticated ability to process all kinds of print, then it seems much more natural that this ability is developed through reading.

To accept that 'children learn to read through reading' does not mean, however, that all we need to do is to give each child some reading materials and sit back and wait for him to learn to read. The child's 'learning through reading' must be a carefully-guided process utilizing carefully-selected materials. This is emphasized in many of the contributions. In point of fact none of the contributors to this volume would advocate any kind of *laissez-faire* approach to the teaching of reading.

It is also worth underlining that the notion that children 'learn to read through reading' does not necessarily entail a so-called informal teaching approach. It may be true that formal teaching methods have often been associated with teaching children to 'bark at print' correctly. But this association – to the extent that it exists – is 'historic accident' rather than methodological necessity. Children's learning to read through reading can be, and in our opinion should be, a systematic, organized process, where the children are guided step by step to higher and higher development of their ability to get meaning from print.

We have discussed our two fundamental principles at some length, mainly in order to underline the importance of founding the teaching of reading on principles. We do not want to suggest that 'our' principles are the only ones on which an approach to the teaching of reading can be founded. But we do believe that any approach to the teaching of reading must be founded on some set of fundamental principles on which decisions regarding the choice of methods and materials can be based.

Once the basic principles have been established, it should be possible to formulate a comprehensive policy of language and reading or, which amounts to practically the same thing, to design a *curriculum for language and reading*. The need for each school to have a comprehensive policy of 'language across the curriculum' was emphasized by the Bullock Committee in one of their principal recommendations. This is a recommendation to which speakers and delegates at the 1977 UKRA Conference probably whole-heartedly subscribe. As a matter of fact, this recommendation – like several of the others made by the Bullock Committee – seems to be so generally accepted that it is taken for granted and not really discussed.

To accept that every school should have a comprehensive policy for language and reading is an important first step, but it is only the first step in a long, long series of steps. It is not much use agreeing that we need a policy, if we have not made clear what we mean by a 'policy' – and what we are going to do with it once we have it. This is the kind of problem we will have to address ourselves to – at a very concrete and practical level – if we want to move ahead 'beyond Bullock'.

Moving ahead
The eleven working parties which met during the Conference produced a total of eighty-seven recommendations, addressed to agencies or categories of people sharing the responsibility for the curriculum in our schools. These recommendations are well worth studying and reflecting upon by all representatives of those parties.

Heads of schools will be reminded of their responsibility to exert pedagogical leadership, and to encourage their staff to cooperate towards well-defined goals.

Teachers are reminded of the importance of open-mindedness and collaboration, and of the need for constant development of their professional skills.

The LEAS are urged to provide leadership and direction in the field of curriculum design and development, and they are reminded of the importance of allocating resources (e.g. staff time) for curriculum development and to organize and monitor the use of these resources.

Publishers of educational materials are asked to establish closer contacts with teachers, and to develop, in cooperation with teachers, new types of reading materials across the curriculum.

Researchers and research bodies are reminded that research in reading, as in any educational area, is worthwhile only if it relates to issues that concern teachers and pupils in schools. And it is pointed out that involving teachers as partners in the research is one of the best ways of ensuring its relevance.

Finally, the UKRA itself is asked to assume its full responsibility as the major professional organization concerned primarily with literacy, and to strengthen its work in various areas: for example, publishing, recruiting members, defining needs for initial and in-service training of teachers, and setting standards of expertise.

All the eighty-seven recommendations should, then, be carefully considered by the respective agencies in their planning for the future. It is also important that these recommendations be further developed and their implications spelt out. The working parties met for three brief sessions during a conference where many activities competed for the delegates' time and interest. In this very limited time the working parties contributed significantly to the identification of major needs, but they obviously did not have time to work out more detailed plans for action.

The recommendations, and this volume as a whole, must be seen as part of a continuous effort to improve the language and reading curriculum. No definite solutions are given and none should be expected, but we hope that enough advice is provided to enable each and everybody to take one or two steps forward, and to assess in what direction the next few steps should be taken.

What primarily seems to be needed at this stage is the translation of recommendations – whether put forward by the Bullock Committee, a UKRA Working Party or some other body – into plans for action. This should involve concerted efforts by representatives of all agencies and bodies concerned with the schooling of our young people. Short-term action plans, i.e. for the next couple of years, are most desperately needed, but plans for a longer time perspective should also be developed.

These action plans must be coordinated at several levels. All teachers – and other staff – concerned with the education of a special category of children within a school need a common action plan for their work. And the school needs a 'master plan' to coordinate the plans of teams of teachers or individual teachers. Groups of neighbouring schools need to plan their catering for the whole population of pupils in an area, particularly with a view to facilitating transitions from school to school. And each LEA must be clear about how it wants to 'deploy its forces' in the struggle for an improved language and reading curriculum which cuts across the traditional compartments of the subject-oriented curriculum.

It is extremely important that any such action plan is genuinely accepted by all those concerned, otherwise it stands little chance of being acted upon. The very essence of an action plan is that it is not merely an expression of what one would like to do, but an outline of what one has *decided to do*. The test of the plan is, then, in the action that follows from it. This in turn means that without some kind of monitoring of action (or lack of action), following the adoption of the plan, one will never know whether or not it has been a successful plan.

Although we cannot here propose detailed action plans for teachers, schools or LEAs, we do believe that a great deal of guidance is needed in this area. The very idea of concerted, co-ordinated planning with the aim of leading directly to action is new to many of those concerned. The individualistic tendency to mind one's own business and not meddle in other people's affairs is often stronger than the sense of solidarity with the system as a whole and the need to integrate one's own efforts with those of other people. What is needed, therefore, is the setting of concrete examples, showing how a curriculum *can* be developed and implemented.

It seems clear to us that the Bullock Committee achieved too little by attempting to achieve too much. The Bullock Report is the most important document of its kind, bringing together a wealth of evidence and informed opinion concerning the theory and practice of teaching reading and other language skills. But in its endeavour to be objective, the Committee somehow succeeded in highlighting the more controversial aspects of the curriculum requirements, but failed to give sufficient emphasis to those very important aspects about which there is little, if any, doubt.

These aspects relate, in particular, to the need for each school – or better still each group of related schools – to so organize its methods and resources that the progress of each of its pupils can be carefully monitored through a planned and structured curriculum. Now this is stated in the Bullock Report, but unfortunately in a way which gives rise to more questions than it solves. One is reminded here of the reaction of a Florida teacher after a lecture outlining the nationwide American *Right to Read* campaign:

For twenty years I've been listening to research on what my problem is, when all the time I knew my problem. I've been waiting for someone to tell me how to solve it. (*St Petersburg Times*, Florida, 20 December 1970)

It is our belief that the Bullock Committee has defined and described most of our problems in this fundamental area of education, but has failed to give sufficient help towards their solution. The brief of the Committee provided a rare opportunity to define authoritatively specific curriculum needs, and to draw up important criteria by which curriculum components can be evaluated. The Bullock Committee saw dangers in publishing an example of a 'policy' for language and reading, because it felt that every school had to develop its own policy for its own unique population of pupils. It is true that there is danger in too much prescription, since a prescribed policy may be implemented half-heartedly – or not at all. But there is even greater danger in lack of guidance, which leaves too much of the burden of curriculum planning to the teacher, and may result in apathy. Every school has similar problems to solve in the formulation of a valuable curriculum for the development of basic language and reading skills, and it is our opinion that very detailed guidance can be given while still leaving ample scope for individual schools to cater for the special needs of their unique groups of pupils.

In his foreword to the Bullock Report, Reg Prentice, then Secretary of State for Education and Science, acknowledges our debt to the Committee. He adds: 'They have given us an authoritative statement which will be of value as a basis for further discussion and development for many years to come.' Some of these years have already come – and gone – and 'further development' is overdue. Moreover, further development is not likely to occur spontaneously, but only as the result of a systematic, organized effort. One way of initiating further development that should, in our opinion, be tried, is the setting up of panels of suitably qualified educationists with the brief to formulate series of curricula appropriate to various levels of language and reading development.

Each panel should develop a model curriculum for a relatively small and well-defined area, and initiate and monitor the implementation of the model curriculum in a number of pilot schools; implementation in this case meaning adoption after adjustment to ocal needs, and *not* acceptance of an externally-imposed curriculum. Taking the Bullock Report as its starting point, this kind of 'further development' would result in the tangible and assessable outcome which is so badly needed in this field.

The model curricula which would be developed and tested by the proposed panels would provide guidance and direction for heads of schools and teachers. They would also provide guidelines for the design and organization of initial and in-service teacher-training courses, and for the production of instructional materials for the development of language and reading skills at all age and ability levels.

Given the kind of high-level support and funding enjoyed by the Bullock Committee, a coordinated, large-scale effort to set up the proposed panels for the development and testing of model curricula could go a long way towards bringing about the long-awaited implementation of the Bullock Report, and towards fulfilling urgent curriculum demands in the field of language and reading.

The contributors

Muriel Buckley
Senior Specialist Teacher
Barking Schools' Psychological Service
Dagenham

Carolyn Burke, Ph.D.
Department of Education
University of Indiana
U.S.A.

Lawrence W. Carrillo, Ph.D.
Department of Education
San Francisco State University
California, U.S.A.

Betty Coody, Ph.D.
Professor of Education
Department of Education
Lamar University
Beaumont, Texas, U.S.A.

Brian Daly
Educational Psychologist
Barking Schools' Psychological Service
Dagenham

James M. Ewing, B.Sc., M.Ed.
Lecturer in Psychology
Dundee College of Education

Kenneth S. Goodman, Ph.D.
Department of Elementary Education
University of Arizona College of Education
U.S.A.

Yetta M. Goodman, Ph.D.
Department of Elementary Education
University of Arizona College of Education
U.S.A.

Hans U. Grundin, Ph.D.
Institute of Educational Technology
The Open University

E. Sheila Harri-Augstein, Ph.D.
Centre for the Study of Human Learning
Brunel University

Norman Hidden, M.A.
Editor of *New Poetry* Magazine
London

Elizabeth Hunter-Grundin, Ph.D.
Senior Lecturer in Reading
Avery Hill College, London

Moira McKenzie, Ph.D.
Director of the Centre for Language in Primary Education
Inner London Education Authority

Michael Marland, CBE, B.A.
Headmaster
Woodberry Down School, London

John E. Merritt, B.A., A.B.Ps.S.
Professor of Educational Studies
The Open University

Joyce M. Morris, B.A., Ph.D.
Language Arts Consultant
London

Bridie Raban, B.A., M.Ed.
Bristol Reading Centre
Avon County

Jessie F. Reid, M.A., M.Ed.
formerly Senior Lecturer at the Centre for Research in
    Educational Sciences
University of Edinburgh

Geoffrey R. Roberts
Faculty of Education
University of Manchester

Vera Southgate, M.A., B.Com.
Senior Lecturer in Curriculum Studies
Faculty of Education
University of Manchester

Margaret D. Spencer
Department of English
University of London Institute of Education

Laurie F. Thomas, Ph.D.
Centre for the Study of Human Learning
Brunel University

Geoff Trickey
Senior Educational Psychologist
Barking Schools' Psychological Service
Dagenham

221